Vegetarian Recipes

My hearse will be followed not by mourning coaches but by herds of oxen, sheep, swine, flocks of poultry and a small travelling aquarium of live fish all wearing white scarves in honour of the man who perished rather than eat his fellow creatures.

George Bernard Shaw

Cookery books published by the National Trust

National Trust Recipes by Sarah Edington

Recipes from the Dairy by Robin Weir and Caroline Liddell with Peter Brears

The Art of Dining by Sara Paston-Williams

A Book of Historical Recipes by Sara Paston-Williams

Jams, Preserves & Edible Gifts by Sara Paston-Williams

Tea-time Recipes by Jane Pettigrew

Vegetarian Recipes

Sarah Edington

THE NATIONAL TRUST

For my family and friends who ate with appreciation and whose comments were always constructive

First published in Great Britain in 1990 by National Trust Enterprises Limited as *The National Trust Book of Healthy Eating*. Reprinted 1991

Revised edition published in Great Britain in 2002 by National Trust Enterprises Limited, 36 Queen Anne's Gate, London SW1H 9AS

http://www.nationaltrust.org.uk/bookshop

Illustrations by Soun Vannithone, except for p.39 by Brian Delf, and p.107 by Claude Page

British Library Cataloguing Publication Data
A Catalogue record for this book is available from the British Library

ISBN 0-7078-0309-8

Designed by Newton Engert Partnership

Phototypeset in Berkeley and Frutiger by SPAN Graphics Limited

Printed and bound in Italy, by G. Canale & Co. S.p.A

Contents

Acknowledgements

My thanks to all the cooks who gave me these recipes

Sopie Blunn	Rita Jones	Joe Shaw
Kaye Bussell	Chris Keating	Joan Simmons
Joe Coombs	David Lee	Julie Simmons
June Cox	Sharon Luke	Di Smallman
Clare Cremin	Annabel Marsh	Maureen Smith
Julie Cullen	Shelagh Matthews	Sheila Stockdale
Ann Denford	Margaret Milner	Valerie Stone
Maureen Dodsworth	Joanne Montgomery	Katherine Taylor
Joan Easterbrook	Carol O'Mahony	Melanie Thomas
Sybil Gill	Theresa Owens	Diana Tilbury
Jonathon Glinos	Rosemary Pannell	Karin Tucker
Harry Hawkins	Anne Parkin	Barbara Twiss
Lesley Hunt	Gillian Pickering	Hillary Watkins
Gillian Hunter	Chris Pritchard	Brenda Watson
Paul Jennings	Shirley Santos	

I would also like to thank Esme Auer, who helped me to write and type the recipes. The late Maggie Black helped me on food history.

We Eat to Live – or Live to Eat?

In the western world these days, few of us eat simply to live. Food *is* necessary for life, but it is also a vital part of social activities. A dish made with carefully chosen ingredients, cooked with attention and eaten by the cook with family or friends, is a pleasure for all.

Our earliest ancestors did, however, eat to live. Avebury in Wiltshire, now protected by the National Trust and English Heritage, is a complex of monuments and earthworks, used as a religious and spiritual centre as long ago as 3700 BC. Excavation and research of the Neolithic stone circles have posed more questions about their presence and purpose, than provided answers about the lives of the men and women who dwelt there. Traditionally it has been assumed that these tribes lived a mainly vegetarian existence with meat and fish appearing as an occasional supplement provided by the hunter in the community. However, a recent study of Neolithic human bones suggests that the people of this period were heavily reliant on both animal meat and by-products and that cereal- and vegetable- based diets didn't evolve until the Iron Age and Romano-British periods, two to three thousand years later. With this history we can see that the British diet has always varied wildly; from the red meat-weighted diet of the Elizabethan courtier or the eighteenth-century gentleman, to the fibre-rich, animal-product-free diets of today's Vegans.

Vegetarian dishes have gained enormously in popularity in the past decade, partly due to the wide variety of vegetables and fruit now available to us. A growing awareness of other food cultures, concerns over diet and anxieties about modern farming methods have all played their part too. All National Trust restaurants offer a vegetarian dish at lunchtime and specialise in cakes and puddings using fresh produce and no additives, such as colouring and chemical flavour-enhancers.

This is a new edition of a collection of recipes from twenty-one National Trust restaurants using a variety of vegetables and fruit, milk products, nuts, flours, pulses, spices and herbs. It is intended for anyone who likes to eat a non-meat meal as part of or all their diet, whether the reason is principle, a positive contribution to well-being or simply because they enjoy vegetarian and fruit-based recipes. Every recipe tastes good – some recipes do use white sugar, butter, alcohol and cream, but they also include fresh vegetables and fruit loaded with vitamins, bran, brown rice, whole-wheat flour and yoghurt.

Some of the soups are substantial enough to make a meal in themselves. Try Country Vegetable Soup from Kedleston or Dame Alice Soup, a hearty and splendid old recipe from Moseley Old Hall. Others are subtle and sophisticated such as Golden Cider Soup from Montacute – it has a lovely colour and delicate aroma. Try Ossum Salad from Buckland Abbey with its interesting ingredients and delightful story behind the odd name. I have included half a dozen pâtés, some served hot with a piquant sauce as a main course, some perfect as an hors-d'œuvre or for a light lunch with toast or crusty bread.

Many National Trust restaurants are lucky enough to be able to use fresh herbs from their own kitchen gardens. Traditional ingredients, such as leeks in Northumberland, carrots in Derbyshire, apples and cider in Herefordshire and Somerset, feature in many recipes. I have selected hearty gratins, hotpots and bakes, as well as sophisticated dishes such as Pinenut and Spinach Jalousie from Charlecote, or Mushroom and Broad Bean Gougère from Cliveden which are spectacular enough for any special occasion. If you are interested in historic recipes, there's a Greate Pye and a Spiced Bean Pottage from Oxburgh.

I couldn't visit National Trust restaurants without sampling some of the puddings and cakes for which they are justly famous. I have restricted the selection, apart from the odd regional biscuit recipe, to fruit- or vegetable-based recipes. Vegetable-based may sound rather odd but you will find an interesting Indian inspired carrot pudding from Claremont, a delicious green and orange speckled Carrot, Courgette and Caraway Cake from Cliveden and a damp and delectable poppy seed cake from Buckland Abbey. There are also tarts and cakes using locally produced apples and cider and scones using fresh herbs and local cheese.

Since these are mostly family recipes, quantities are also family size and will serve four to six people according to appetite. Where cakes are concerned, I have given a tin size. Some of the soups and salads were difficult to reduce to one-meal quantities and you may well find that they will feed more hungry mouths at another meal the next day! Eggs are all standard size 3 unless otherwise indicated. If no specific type of sugar is given, use caster sugar. I have given cooking times and temperatures but these do vary from oven to oven, so please regard them more as an indication than an order.

Cakes and sponge puddings should be taken out of their tins and cooled on a wire tray after cooking, and stored only after they are cold. Similarly, all biscuits should be cooled on a wire tray and put in a tin only when completely cold. When re-heating dishes, they should be heated until they are piping hot throughout.

Interspersed with the recipes, you will find quotations, anecdotes, the odd piece of poetry, household hints and old remedies. Most are connected with vegetables or vegetarians in some way. We are by no means the first generation to be interested in finding alternatives to meat – I hope this book will help to make that quest more enjoyable.

When did we start eating that?

British farmers of the first millennium AD raised wheat and barley, peas and broad beans. Otherwise the vegetables eaten were collected from the wild and might have included delicacies such as samphire and sea kale from the coast as well as fungi, nettles, dandelion and wood sorrel. Mustard, poppy seeds, and wild garlic were used as flavourings. All the fruit and nuts eaten belonged to wild species. Hazelnuts were particularly popular as they could be stored throughout the winter months, otherwise fruits and nuts were eaten in season. Acorns, sloes, crab apples, blackberries, elderberries, strawberries and rosehips have all been found at prehistoric sites.

The coming of the Romans to Britain in AD43 changed the lives of ordinary people irrevocably, with new laws, new gods and new varieties of food. Onion, cabbage, leek, lettuce, endive, turnip, courgette, radish, apple, walnut and sweet chestnut, were all introduced. Interested and imaginative cooks, the Romans often flavoured their sauces with the pot-herbs that we use today, such as fennel, mint, thyme, garlic, rosemary, sage and sweet marjoram.

In the Middle Ages, only the rich ate imported delicacies like oranges and apricots, dates and figs. When the vegetables from the New World began to arrive in Elizabethan England, again it was the wealthy who could afford them: potatoes from Chile, kidney beans from Peru and tomatoes or 'love apples' from Mexico. Sir Walter Raleigh wowed the court of Elizabeth I with the sweet potato from Virginia. But it took generations for these exotics to become staples. Even the lowly potato was not eaten by all classes until the end of the eighteenth century.

Nowadays, we can eat what we want in any season. Food wings its way around the world and onto our plates; avocados from Israel, green beans from Kenya, asparagus from California. We take it all for granted but is the taste better than the wild vegetables and fruits, picked and eaten in season that sustained our forefathers?

Please Sir – I want some more?

'"What!" said the master [Mr Bumble], at length in a faint voice. "Please, sir," replied Oliver, "I want some more".'

This famous episode is familiar to all who know the story of *Oliver Twist*. The 'thin gruel, with onion twice a week', must have seemed appetising to a starving child. But was Charles Dickens fair to workhouse cooks? Possibly not; in the eighteenth and nineteenth centuries, inmates of the workhouses, nourished on a diet that might include milk porridge, bread, cheese, beer, root vegetables and meat were sometimes eating a more varied diet than their contemporaries in the working community.

The day usually began with oat porridge made with milk or water accompanied by milk, broth or beer. Suppers were usually porridge or bread also accompanied by broth or beer, but at midday the diet was much more varied. Most workhouses provided two or three meat meals a week: boiled beef or mutton served with vegetables, raised in the workhouse garden, bread, dumplings and suet puddings. On the other days hasty pudding (steamed suet), crowdy (soft cheese eaten with sugar), frumenty (hulled wheat in milk), bread and cheese, rice milk (stewed rice in milk) or pease pottage (dried peas stewed, rather like mushy peas) might form the meal.

Nutritious but dull, meals brightened up at festival times: roast beef and a pound of spice cake at Christmas, veal and bacon at Easter and Whitsuntide in Leeds; plum puddings instead of spice cake in Sheffield. Otherwise only the sick ate delicacies such as sugar given to children with smallpox, tea, brandy or raisin wine given to women 'lying-in'. All these feature in accounts from the infirmaries.

But despite the better diet and living conditions, the workhouse, with its sense of personal failure and loss of freedom, was seen as the last resort. Ruthlessly impersonal regimes separated husband, wife and children. Inmates were further segregated into two groups: 'Blameless and Deserving', the old or sick, and 'Idle and Profligate', the unemployed. Schedules were monotonous and punishing. Workhouses operated well into the twentieth century, until the 1920s when most institutions were handed over to local authorities and continued more benignly as hospitals or homes for the homeless or elderly.

If you would like to see what life in the workhouse was like, go and visit the Thurgaton Hundred Incorporated Workhouse, built in 1824 at Southwell in Nottinghamshire. The collection of buildings includes men's, women's and children's wings, an infirmary, a mortuary, washhouse and stables. They probably constitute the best preserved workhouse in England where, since 1997, the Trust has been at work to protect and restore them, allowing us a glimpse into the hard life that the less successful of our ancestors had to endure. The workhouse opens from Easter 2002.

Conversions

The following approximate conversions are used in this book

½ oz	12 g	1 teaspoon	5 ml	
1 oz	25 g	1 dessertspoon	10 ml	
2 oz	50 g	1 tablespoon	15 ml	
3 oz	75 g	1 fluid oz	30 ml	
4 oz	115 g	4 fluid oz	100 ml	
5 oz	140 g	5 fluid oz	125 ml	
6 oz	170 g	8 fluid oz	225 ml	
7 oz	200 g	10 fluid oz	300 ml	
8 oz	225 g	12 fluid oz	360 ml	
12 oz	350 g	15 fluid oz	450 ml	
1 lb	450 g			
1½ lb	675 g	¼ pint	150 ml	
2 lb	900 g	½ pint	250 ml	
		1 pint	500 ml	
¼ in	6 mm	1½ pints	750 ml	
½ in	1·25 cm	1¾ pints	1 litre	
¾ in	2 cm	2 pints	1·25 litres	
1 in	2·5 cm			
1½ in	4 cm	gas mark 1	275°F	140°C
2 in	5 cm	gas mark 2	300°F	150°C
6 in	15 cm	gas mark 3	325°F	160°C
7 in	18 cm	gas mark 4	350°F	180°C
8 in	20 cm	gas mark 5	375°F	190°C
9 in	23 cm	gas mark 6	400°F	200°C
10 in	25 cm	gas mark 7	425°F	220°C
12 in	30·5 cm	gas mark 8	450°F	230°C

American Equivalents

Dry Measures

1 US cup	=	50 g	=	2 oz of:	breadcrumbs; fresh cake crumbs
1 US cup	=	75 g	=	3 oz of:	rolled oats
1 US cup	=	90 g	=	$3\frac{1}{2}$ oz of:	desiccated coconut; ground almonds
1 US cup	=	100 g	=	4 oz of:	grated hard cheese; walnut pieces; drinking chocolate; icing sugar; cocoa; flaked almonds; pasta; frozen peas
1 US cup	=	125 g	=	5 oz of:	white flour; self-raising flour; currants; muesli; chopped dates; ground roasted almonds
1 US cup	=	150 g	=	$5\frac{1}{2}$ oz of:	wholemeal flour; raisins; cornflour
1 US cup	=	175 g	=	6 oz of:	apricots; mixed peel; sultanas
1 US cup	=	200 g	=	7 oz of:	caster sugar; soft brown sugar; demerara sugar; glacé cherries; lentils; long grain and brown rice;
1 US cup	=	225 g	=	$\frac{1}{2}$ lb of:	cream cheese; cottage cheese
1 US cup	=	300 g	=	11 oz of:	mincemeat; marmalade
1 US cup	=	350 g	=	12 oz of:	syrup; treacle; jam

Liquid Measures

$\frac{1}{4}$ US cup		= 60 ml	=	2 fluid oz
1 US cup		= 240 ml	=	8 fluid oz
2 US cups (1 US pint)		= 480 ml	=	16 fluid oz

Butter, Lard and Margarine Measures

$\frac{1}{4}$ stick		= 25 g	=	2 level tablespoons	=	1 oz
1 stick ($\frac{1}{2}$ US cup)		= 100 g	=	8 level tablespoons	=	4 oz

Information very kindly provided by the Good Housekeeping Institution

Berrington Hall

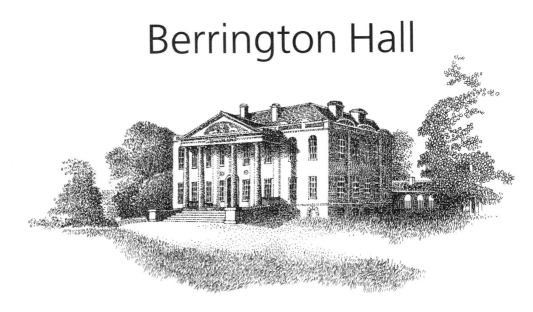

Herefordshire is one of England's most beautiful, unspoilt and uncrowded counties: Berrington Hall, an unpretentiously elegant house, lies in rolling hills north of Leominster. The site of the house is wonderful, which is not surprising as it was chosen and later landscaped with the help of Lancelot 'Capability' Brown.

Designed by Henry Holland in 1778 and finished in 1783, the house is encased in dark red local stone which gives the exterior a slightly austere air, but the interiors provide a complete contrast. The principal rooms have wonderfully delicate ceilings, in particular the Drawing Room, where plaster seahorses and cherubs cavort amongst flowers and leaves, all painted in pastels which have faded to subtly satisfactory blues and lavenders. There is an exquisite Boudoir, a fine Library with interesting ceiling paintings of eminent literary Englishmen, a workmanlike Business Room, a handsome, airy staircase hall, and a cool, marble entrance hall.

On the walls hang portraits of those associated with Berrington, amongst them Thomas Harley, Lord Mayor of London in 1767, who built it, and his daughter Anne, who inherited the house and married George, son of Admiral Rodney. In the Dining Room are four huge dramatic pictures of sea battles in which the Admiral triumphed. During the twentieth century the house was owned by the Cawley family which is remembered by portraits, photographs, mementos and toys.

The house was designed and built without a lavatory or bathroom: chamberpots had to be kept behind the shutters, and hip baths were filled with water carried by servants. Their world is entered across the courtyard on the east side of the house, where there is a Victorian laundry with huge drying racks and mangles, a pretty tiled dairy and the Servants' Hall, a large light room with a great dresser and black-leaded range. On the walls are old photographs, menus and a huge ox's head with the following inscription:

> This ox with six wether sheep and a quantity of bread and cider was given to the poor of the Berrington Estates on the arrival of Lord Rodney with his Bride at Berrington – September 12, 1850.

This is now the restaurant where you will find many local Herefordshire dishes. In the autumn, for instance, you can sample Cat's Head Pye made from Cat's Head Apples grown in the historic apple orchard. Refreshed and restored, do find a few minutes to visit the gardens. The orchard replaces the old kitchen beds within the Walled Garden and you will not only find Cat's Head Apples here but the National Collection of Herefordshire and Marches Apples.

At the other end of the street, at the junction with the Pointe St Eustache, the entrance to the Rue Rambuteau was blocked by a barricade of orange pumpkins, set out in twin rows, displaying their swollen bellies. A basket of onions, their skins like polished bronze, a pile of blood-red tomatoes, a mound of faded yellow cucumbers, a brace of purple aubergines added intermittent flashes of colour. Meanwhile fat, black radishes, draped as if in mourning, cast a funereal darkness amid this vibrant scene of joyous awakening.

Emile Zola *Le Ventre de Paris* 1873

Celery and Stilton Soup

1 medium head of celery, chopped
1 medium onion, chopped
50g (2oz) butter
500ml (1 pint) vegetable stock
salt and pepper

170g (6oz) Stilton cheese
15ml (3 teaspoons) cornflour
400ml (¾ pint) milk
celery leaves, chopped

Place the chopped celery and onion in a saucepan and sauté gently in the butter until soft, with a lid on the pan. Pour in the vegetable stock and season with salt and pepper. Bring to the boil and simmer for 20 minutes. Liquidise in a food processor or blender and return to the pan with the crumbled or grated Stilton. In a cup or small bowl cream the cornflour with a little cold milk and add to the soup with the balance of the milk. Reheat gently, but do not boil, and check the seasoning. Garnish the soup with a few chopped celery leaves and crushed black peppercorns.

Celery and Stilton are both strong flavours; cooked this way the soup enhances both.

Tomato, Onion and Ginger Soup

1 large onion, chopped
30ml (2 tablespoons) sunflower oil
2·5cm (1in) fresh root ginger, finely
    chopped, or pinch of ground
    ginger

750ml (1½ pints) vegetable stock
400g (14oz) tin tomatoes
10ml (1 dessertspoon) tomato purée
fresh herbs of your choice
salt and pepper

In a large saucepan sauté the chopped onion in the sunflower oil together with the ginger until soft and transparent. Add the balance of the ingredients and bring to the boil. Simmer for around 20 minutes, then liquidise in a food processor. Before serving, reheat and adjust the seasoning if necessary.

If you wish, this soup can be thickened with a little cornflour. Do try to obtain fresh ginger as it gives this soup a fresh and unusual tang, but it is important to chop it very finely.

Berrington Homity Pies

300g (10oz) wholemeal pastry

Filling

350g (12oz) potatoes
450g (1lb) onions, chopped
45ml (3 tablespoons) vegetable oil
25g (1oz) butter
15ml (1 tablespoon) parsley, chopped

115g (4oz) Cheddar cheese, grated
2 cloves garlic, crushed
15ml (1 tablespoon) milk
salt and pepper to taste

Preheat oven: 220°C, 425°F; gas mark 7.

Roll out the pastry and line six 10cm (4in) individual tins. Boil the potatoes until tender. Sauté the onions in the oil until soft but not coloured. Then combine the potatoes and onions, add butter, parsley, half the cheese, garlic and milk, and season to taste. Cool, then fill the cases. Sprinkle with the remaining cheese and bake in the oven for 20 minutes, until golden.

This Cranks-inspired recipe is a great favourite at Berrington.

Macaroni Cheese and Tomato Bake

Makes four dishes

225g (8oz) dried macaroni
1 medium onion, chopped
15ml (1 tablespoon) oil
400g (14oz) tin tomatoes, drained
10ml (1 dessertspoon) tomato purée
dried mixed herbs or fresh basil

salt and pepper
75g (3oz) butter
50g (2oz) plain flour
5ml (1 teaspoon) mustard
400ml (¾ pint) milk
225g (8oz) cheese, grated

Preheat oven: 200°C, 400°F; gas mark 6.

Boil the macaroni according to the instructions on the packet and drain well.

Sauté the chopped onion gently in a little oil and add the drained tomatoes, tomato purée and plenty of herbs. Cook together for a few minutes, breaking the tomatoes with a wooden spoon and season to taste.

Make a cheese sauce: melt the butter in a saucepan, stir in the flour with a teaspoon of mustard and cook for a minute before pouring in the milk. Stirring all the time, bring to the boil and add 170g (6oz) of the grated cheese.

Stir the tomatoes into the cooked macaroni and spoon into individual baking dishes. Cover each portion with the cheese sauce and sprinkle some grated cheese on top. Bake in the oven for 20 minutes or until golden brown.

Wholewheat Pancakes with Ratatouille or Mushroom Filling

Makes six–eight pancakes

Pancake Batter
50g (2oz) plain wholewheat flour
pinch of salt
2 eggs

15ml (1 tablespoon) oil
150ml (¼ pint) milk
oil for frying

Ratatouille Filling
1 onion, coarsely chopped
2 cloves of garlic, crushed
1 small aubergine, diced into chunks
2 courgettes, sliced
115g (4oz) mushrooms, sliced

60ml (4 tablespoons) olive oil
400g (14oz) tin tomatoes
5ml (1 teaspoon) mixed herbs
salt and freshly ground black pepper

Mushroom Filling
75g (3oz) butter
25g (1oz) plain flour
250ml (½ pint) milk

225g (8oz) mushrooms, chopped
salt and pepper
fresh herbs

Make the batter by placing all the ingredients into a food processor and blending for a few seconds until smooth. If you do not have a food processor, put the flour and salt into a bowl and gradually beat in the eggs. Continue beating while adding the oil and milk until a smooth consistency is reached. Brush a small frying pan with oil and make the pancakes in the usual way. Stack them on a plate and keep warm while you prepare the filling.

Ratatouille Filling
Use the ratatouille recipe from Montacute (p.96)

Mushroom Filling
Make a white sauce by melting half the butter, then stirring in and cooking the flour for a few seconds. Gradually add the milk, stirring all the time, until the mixture comes to the boil and a thick sauce is made. Sauté the mushrooms in the remaining butter and add to the white sauce with seasoning and fresh herbs.

Place a good tablespoon of filling on each pancake and roll up. Serve immediately or re-heat in the oven brushed with a little melted butter.

Herefordshire Cider Cake

225g (8oz) caster sugar
225g (8oz) butter
450g (1lb) self-raising flour
5ml (1 teaspoon) ground ginger

2·5ml (½ teaspoon) ground nutmeg
4 eggs
250ml (½ pint) cider

Preheat oven: 160°C, 325°F; gas mark 3.

Grease and line a 23cm (9in) cake tin. Cream together the sugar and butter until light and fluffy. Sieve the flour and spices into the mixture and gently fold in with a wooden spoon. In a separate bowl whisk together the eggs and cider, then stir them into the cake mixture. Spoon into the cake tin and bake in the centre of the oven for approximately 45 minutes. Turn out on to a wire tray to cool before glazing with glacé icing made with (115–170g [4–6oz] icing sugar to 15–30ml [1–2 tablespoons] cider).

At Berrington this is, of course, made with cider from local Herefordshire apples.

The Cat's Head Apple is named for the distinctive marking on its base. Herefordshire tradition says that this apple is the original used for the 'Ploughman's Lunch'. Nowadays a 'pub ploughman's' usually consists of bread, cheese, apple and pickle. However, Herefordshire farm labourers carried with them as their midday 'bait' or snack an apple dumpling made from this specific large green cooking apple. Herefordshire has always been a famous apple-growing area but many old varieties were falling out of use and threatened with extinction. Berrington rescued apples such as 'Herefordshire Beefing' a small dark, crimson apple dating back to the 1700s and 'Lady's Finger' or 'Hereford East' a slender yellow cider apple first bred in 1884. They now flourish in the Walled Garden together with pears, morello cherries, figs, mulberries and quinces.

Box Hill

Box Hill is a commanding chalk promontory of woodland and open rolling downland with a steep 400 foot drop to the River Mole on the south and west. One of the best-known summits of the North Downs, it provides on a clear day a vista across the Weald to the tower on Leith Hill (also in the care of the National Trust) and even to Chanctonbury Ring 25 miles to the south and Windsor Castle to the north west. Jane Austen chose the hill as the site of a picnic in *Emma*:

> Emma had never been to Box Hill; she wished to see what every body found so well worth seeing, and she and Mr Weston had agreed to choose some fine morning and drive thither. Two or three more of the chosen only were to be admitted to join them, and it was to be done in a quiet, unpretending elegant way . . .

Like Jane Austen's Emma Woodhouse in 1816, I, too, in 1988 had never been to Box Hill on the edge of the North Downs, though I already knew I would find there fine views, pleasant walks and interesting trees, plants, birds, animals and insects.

In Emma's day, excursions to Box Hill were by carriage, but with the coming of the railway in 1860, the fresh air, lovely woods and exceptional views were accessible to everyone and Box Hill became, and still is, a great favourite with Londoners of all ages.

In all seasons, the walker will find chalkland flowers blooming at their feet, delicate cowslips, pyramid and bee orchids, mallow and harebells. In the summer, butterflies with enchanting names flutter amongst the grasses: silverspotted skipper, chalkhill blues and marbled whites. The bird life is wonderful; tiny tits co-exist with woodpeckers, tree creepers, wood-pigeons and tawny owls. A flash of blue down by the river is a kingfisher, the shyest of birds. The lucky visitor may also catch a glimpse of the shyest of animals, the roe deer, browsing in the open woodland in the misty early morning or at dusk. Many of these plants and creatures are becoming increasingly rare with the encroachment of building and pollution, making Box Hill an important reserve and a welcome haven for the natural world.

Walking, kite-flying and birdwatching all encourage healthy appetites. High on the hill is the Old Fort, a legacy of a ring of forts constructed between 1893 and 1902 for the defence of London. The low white building with wooden verandah is peaceful now and, as well as a shop and information centre, contains a servery open every day of the year. Hot home-made soups and savoury scones, bread pudding and well-filled sandwiches are all made on the premises. Box Hill Big Biscuits, chocolate with chocolate chips, ginger with raisins, baked fresh to recipes invented on the spot, will re-energise the most exhausted walker.

Curried Parsnip Soup

30 ml (2 tablespoons) sunflower or olive oil
450 g (1 lb) parsnips, peeled and chopped into chunks
10 ml (2 teaspoons) Korma curry paste

750 ml (1½ pints) vegetable stock – see recipe page 23 or make up from vegetable bouillon powder or stock cubes
salt and pepper to taste

Sauté the chopped parsnips gently in the oil until they are soft. Add the curry paste and cook for a further three minutes. Add the vegetable stock. Stir well, bring to the boil and simmer for about 30 minutes. Liquidise the mixture, add salt and pepper to taste.

Serve piping hot with a fresh and generously buttered cheese and herb scone as accompaniment.

Cheese and Herb Scones

450g (1 lb) self-raising flour sifted
12g (½oz) baking powder
5ml (1 teaspoon) salt
115g (4oz) mature Cheddar cheese, grated

12g (½oz) mixed dried herbs
50g (2oz) baking margarine or butter
225ml (8fl oz) milk and water (half and half)

Preheat oven: 180°C, 350°F; gas mark 4.

Either grease and flour a metal baking sheet or line it with baking parchment.

Put flour, baking powder, salt, half the grated cheese and the dried herbs in a large bowl. Rub in margarine or butter into the dried ingredients until the mixture resembles breadcrumbs. Make a well in the centre and add the milk and water slowly and knead until you have a soft dough. Roll out the dough and cut into 12 × 7·5 cm, (3 inch) rounds. Sprinkle the rest of the cheese on the top of each scone. Bake for approximately 17 minutes.

Vegetable Stock

2 large leeks
2 large carrots
2 large onions
1 head of celery

5ml (1 teaspoon) of salt
8 peppercorns
2·5 litres (4 pints) of water

Peel as necessary and chop finely all the vegetables. Put in a saucepan, add water, salt and peppercorns. Bring to the boil and simmer uncovered for 20 minutes. Allow to stand until cool, then strain and use as necessary.

This stock will keep well in the fridge for at least two weeks. You can also freeze it.

Cheese and Celery Soup

1 head of celery	750 ml (1½ pints) vegetable stock
1 large carrot	salt and pepper
1 large onion	170 g (6 oz) Cheddar cheese, grated

Trim the celery and slice, peel and chop the carrot and onion and place in a saucepan with the vegetable stock and seasoning. Bring to the boil, reduce the heat and simmer for about 1 hour, until the vegetables are quite soft. Purée the soup in a blender or food processor. Reheat in the saucepan and add the grated Cheddar cheese. Serve with the leaves from the heart of the celery.

The chef recommends that this soup be eaten to warm the bones on a cold day in front of the fire with a glass of port and a fresh wholemeal bread roll!

Spinach Tortellini with Tomato and Basil Sauce

350 g (12 oz) fresh or frozen spinach tortellini

Tomato and Basil Sauce

1 medium onion	3–4 stalks of fresh basil leaves,
2 cloves of garlic	chopped
30 ml (2 tablespoons) oil	Worcestershire sauce
400 g (14 oz) tin Italian plum	salt and pepper
tomatoes	

Cook the tortellini as directed on the packet.

To make the sauce, chop the onion and garlic and sauté in a saucepan with the oil and cook over a medium heat until the onion is soft and transparent. Add the tomatoes, basil leaves, a few drops of Worcestershire sauce and seasoning and cook for around 20 minutes, stirring every now and then to break up the tomatoes until the sauce has thickened. Process lightly in a blender or food processor until the sauce is coarsely chopped and still retains some texture. Pour over and combine with the pasta and serve with a green salad.

Fresh Fruit Kebabs

Strawberries	Pineapple
Chunks of apple, pears or bananas dipped first in lemon juice	Melon
Cherries (stoned)	Mangoes

Dip
small pot of Greek yoghurt
sugar to taste

Thread 3 or 4 different fruits on a 15 cm (6 in) stick. Arrange them in a circle on a large platter decorated with, say, vine leaves. Place in the centre a small bowl of Greek yoghurt mixed with soft brown sugar to taste. Guests then help themselves and use the yoghurt and sugar as a dip.

This can be particularly colourful and perfect for a crowd.

Carrot and Walnut Loaf

140 g (5 oz) butter	170 g (6 oz) raisins or dates
5 ml (1 teaspoon) vanilla essence	115 g (4 oz) chopped walnuts
170 g (6 oz) caster sugar	300 g (10 oz) self-raising flour
30 ml (2 tablespoons) golden syrup	2·5 ml (½ teaspoon) ground nutmeg
2 eggs	2·5 ml (½ teaspoon) cinnamon
225 g (8 oz) carrots, grated	

Preheat oven: 180°C, 350°F; gas mark 4.

Grease and line a 900 g (2 lb) loaf tin with greased paper. Cream together the butter, essence and sugar until light and fluffy. Add the golden syrup and beat in the eggs one at a time until well mixed. The mixture may look curdled at this stage but do not worry. Stir in the carrots, raisins and walnuts and gently fold in the flour and spices. Turn into the loaf tin and bake in the oven for 1¼ hours. Leave for 5 minutes before turning out. Serve in buttered slices.

This loaf will keep for about 1 week in a tin or wrapped in foil and will also freeze well.

Apricot and Almond Shortcake

300g (10oz) self-raising flour
140g (5oz) butter
115g (4oz) caster sugar
1 egg
15ml (1 tablespoon) lemon juice

15–30ml (1–2 tablespoons) milk (optional)
170g (6oz) apricot jam
1 egg white, lightly beaten
25g (1oz) halved almonds

Preheat oven: 180°C, 350°F; gas mark 4.

Well grease a 20cm (8in) flan tin. Sift the flour into a large bowl and rub in the butter to resemble fine breadcrumbs. Stir in the sugar, egg and lemon juice and draw together to make a light, manageable dough; use a little milk as well if necessary. Place in a polythene bag in the fridge to rest for approximately 30 minutes. Divide dough in half and roll out one half between two sheets of cling film; this makes it much easier to handle. Press it evenly into the base of the tin and slightly draw it up the sides. Heat the jam and spread it over the dough, leaving a small clear margin around the edge. Roll out the remaining dough and place over the jam, pressing the edges firmly together. Brush with the lightly beaten egg white and decorate with the halved almonds. Bake for approximately 30 minutes, or until golden and firm and leave to cool for 10 minutes before turning out.

No fresh fruit or vegetables in this, but it is economical, crisp and good warm or cold. This shortcake will keep for around 3 days and is also suitable for freezing.

Buckland Abbey

Deep in the lush green valleys that separate Devon from Cornwall lies Buckland Abbey. It is a wonderfully peaceful place now, but it has not always been so; during its long history, the fortunes of its owners have been caught up in some of the more turbulent events of medieval and Tudor England.

In the Middle Ages, Buckland was a great Cistercian monastery, a self-sufficient community founded in 1278 by Amicia, Countess of Devon and endowed with over 20,000 acres of land which were farmed by the monks. Their success can be measured by the size of the Great Barn, bigger than the Abbey Church itself, which was built to store produce from the farms. Eight centuries on, it is still an awesome experience to stand in this huge building.

Dissolved by Henry VIII in 1539, the Abbey was bought by Sir Richard Grenville, whose son Roger lived there until he was drowned with 500 of his men in the ill-fated *Mary Rose*. His heir, the Richard Grenville of *Revenge* fame, completed and converted the Abbey buildings into a fine country house. The splendid Great Hall, has, high on its walls, spectacular plasterwork showing vivid allegorical scenes, including a resting knight, his shield and skull hung above him on the 'tree of life'.

There was a disastrous fire here in 1938 but luckily the plaster-work survived, as did the beautiful oak panelling in the Drake

Chamber. Buckland Abbey's most famous owner was Sir Francis Drake, Queen Elizabeth's favourite buccaneer and explorer, and, of course, the man who played a leading role in the English fleet that defeated the Spanish Armada, once he had finished his game of bowls on Plymouth Hoe. Distant relations of Drake continued to live at Buckland until the twentieth century, a Georgian Sir Francis introducing an elegant staircase and fitting out a handsome dining-room. There are interesting exhibitions to visit on Drake, his contemporaries and his career as well as the Abbey itself through the ages.

Stroll back past the Great Barn, the sweet-smelling herb garden and the Linhay, to the long building on your right opposite the Ox Shed, which was the Guesthouse. Now it houses a beautiful restaurant – a long low room with white-washed walls and two great fireplaces at either end, full of flowers. Fennel, sage, thyme, tarragon and other herbs picked fresh from the garden enhance the delicious and unusual recipes you will find here. Try the Spinach and Cream Cheese Pâté or the unusual salads. The hot dishes are substantial and imaginative, and at coffee or tea time, the poppy-seed cake must not be missed.

Sir Francis Drake's sailors were chiefly provisioned on biscuit, salt beef and beer when at sea: 450g (1lb) biscuit and 4.5 litres (1 gallon) beer a day, 2 pieces salt beef or ¼ stockfish or pieces of saltfish on four days of the week with 125–225g (4–8oz) cheese and butter on the other days, supplemented by any fruit, vegetables or fresh meat the captain could procure.

This diet, with its absence of fresh vegetables and fruit, brought on scurvy: 'swollen limbs with haemorrhages under the skin, and foul mouths with swollen, ulcerated and bleeding gums.' Sir Richard Hawkins, who set sail for the South Seas in 1593 and was particularly struck by scurvy among his men, knew of the use of oranges and lemons, but believed the primary cause to be 'the ayre of the land – for the sea is natural for fishe – and the land for men'.

Spinach and Cream Cheese Pâté

450g (1 lb) frozen spinach, defrosted and drained well
3 hard-boiled eggs
225g (8oz) cream cheese
45ml (3 tablespoons) double cream
10ml (1 dessertspoon) Worcestershire sauce
salt and pepper

Put everything in a food processor and blend until smooth. Check the seasoning and pack into 6 ramekin dishes. Chill before serving. This pâté will keep for several days in the fridge.

An unusual first course, or serve with French/granary bread and a salad as a light meal.

Ossum Salad

225g (8oz) tinned or cooked red kidney beans
45ml (3 tablespoons) French dressing
1 small onion, finely chopped
4 sticks celery, finely chopped
1 small cauliflower broken into florets
½ red pepper cut into strips
½ green pepper cut into strips
150ml (¼ pint) soured cream or yoghurt
salt and pepper

Heat the beans gently, then pour over them the French dressing while they are still warm. When they have cooled down, add the remaining ingredients and gently mix everything together. Chill and serve.

It is so called because the original writer of the recipe was visiting American friends when this salad was served. Their son declared, 'Gee Mom, this is an ossum salad'. Intrigued by the name the writer enquired for the recipe, to be told the young man had in fact said the salad was AWESOME! It was therefore always named Ossum Salad.

Carrot, Raisin and Sesame Seed Salad

6 carrots	orange or lemon juice dressing
75g (3oz) raisins	lemon twists for garnish
25g (1oz) sesame seeds	

Coarsely grate the carrots and mix in the raisins and sesame seeds. Garnish with lemon twists and pour over an orange or lemon juice dressing. The Fresh Orange Dressing from Kedleston (p.84) is delicious with this salad.

Cauliflower Salad

1 medium cauliflower cut into florets	15ml (1 tablespoon) tomato purée
45ml (3 tablespoons) mayonnaise	dash of Worcestershire sauce
30ml (2 tablespoons) double cream	salt and pepper

Place cauliflower florets in a bowl. Mix together the balance of the ingredients for a dressing and pour over the florets and garnish with parsley and freshly milled black pepper.

Cucumber and Dill Salad with a Honey, Lemon and Lime Dressing

1 cucumber	30ml (2 tablespoons) fresh dill, chopped (if fresh not available, use slightly reduced quantity of dried)
salt and pepper	

Dressing

15ml (1 tablespoon) lemon juice	15ml (1 tablespoon) lime juice (use another lemon if not available)
30ml (2 tablespoons) runny honey	

Slice the cucumber and season with salt and pepper. Add half the chopped dill and let it stand for approximately ¾ hour in a cool place. Drain off any liquid and pour over the dressing. Garnish with the remaining dill. You will need to serve this with a slotted spoon.

The sweet and sour combination of this salad is unusual and refreshing.

Pasta Salad

225g (8oz) pasta shells
1 bunch of spring onions
½ green pepper

French dressing
edible flowers such as nasturtiums
or violets

Cook the pasta shells according to instructions in boiling water and drain well. Chop the spring onions and pepper, add them to the pasta and pour over the French dressing. Garnish the salad with flowers.

Orange and Nut Roast with Yoghurt and Orange Sauce

Orange and Nut Roast

25g (1oz) butter
1 medium onion, chopped
2 large eggs (size 1 or 2)
115g (4oz) brown breadcrumbs
5ml (1 teaspoon) mixed herbs
225g (8oz) chopped mixed nuts
grated zest of an orange

1 small parsnip, cooked and mashed
juice of an orange made up to
    250ml (½ pint) of liquid with
    vegetable stock
5ml (1 teaspoon) yeast extract
salt and freshly milled pepper

Yoghurt and Orange Sauce

180ml (6fl oz) natural yoghurt
30ml (2 tablespoons) double cream,
    lightly whipped

zest and juice of one orange
50g (2oz) onion, finely chopped

Preheat oven: 180°C, 350°F; gas mark 4.

Sauté onion in butter until soft. Leave aside to cool a little. Beat eggs in a bowl large enough to take all the ingredients. Add breadcrumbs, herbs, nuts, orange zest and onion, mix well and add finally the mashed parsnip. Dissolve the yeast extract in the vegetable stock and juice and add to the other ingredients. Taste and season accordingly with salt and pepper.

Prepare a 450g (1lb) loaf tin by lining the base and sides with silicon paper. Then turn the mixture into the lined tin and press down well. Cover with foil and cook for 30–40 minutes. Remove foil and cook for a further 10 minutes. Turn out, eat hot or cold with Yoghurt and Orange Sauce, which is made by simply mixing the ingredients together.

Optionally 50g (2oz) of grated mature Cheddar can be added to the roast mixture.

Brazil Nut Roast

25g (1 oz) butter
1 medium onion, chopped
2 large eggs
115g (4 oz) brown breadcrumbs
2·5ml (½ teaspoon) dried basil
2·5ml (½ teaspoon) dried marjoram
225g (8 oz) chopped Brazil nuts

1 small cooked swede, mashed
150ml (¼ pint) vegetarian stock
150ml (¼ pint) red wine
5ml (1 teaspoon) yeast extract
15ml (1 tablespoon) peanut butter
salt and freshly milled pepper

Red Wine Sauce

15ml (1 tablespoon) oil
1 medium onion, peeled and finely
  chopped
1 clove of garlic, crushed
2·5ml (½ teaspoon) mixed herbs

250ml (½ pint) vegetable stock
150ml (¼ pint) red wine
salt and freshly milled pepper
arrowroot or cornflour to thicken

Preheat oven: 180°C, 350°F; gas mark 4.

Sauté onion in butter until soft. Leave aside to cool a little. Beat eggs in a bowl large enough to take all the ingredients. Add breadcrumbs, herbs, nuts and finally the mashed swede and mix well. Dissolve the yeast extract in the wine and stock and add to the other ingredients together with the peanut butter. Season to taste with salt and pepper.

Prepare a 450g (1 lb) loaf tin by lining base and sides with silicon paper. Then turn the mixture into the lined tin and press down well. Cover with foil and cook for 30–40 minutes. Remove foil and cook for a further 10 minutes. Turn out, serve with Red Wine Sauce.

To make the sauce, sauté in the oil the onion and garlic in a small saucepan until soft but not coloured. Add herbs, stock and wine and simmer until liquid is reduced by approximately one third. Season with salt and pepper and thicken to taste with a little arrowroot or cornflour.

This nut roast would make a good vegetarian Christmas dish.

Vegetable Croustade

For the Base

50g (2oz) almonds
25g (1oz) sesame seeds
50g (2oz) walnuts
25g (1oz) cheese grated

75g (3oz) breadcrumbs
5ml (1 teaspoon) mixed herbs
salt and pepper
45ml (3 tablespoons) oil/butter

Topping

75g (3oz) cheese, grated
75g (3oz) breadcrumbs

25g (1oz) sesame seeds

Vegetable Mix

115g (4oz) butter
2 medium-sized onions, chopped
450g (1lb) vegetables (peppers,
 celery, carrots, cauliflower, leeks,
 courgettes), chopped
salt and pepper

2·5ml (½ teaspoon) grated nutmeg
15ml (1 tablespoon) soy sauce
115g (4oz) mushrooms
20ml (2 dessertspoons) flour
250–400ml (½–¾ pint) milk

Preheat oven 180°C, 350°F; gas mark 4.

Coarsely chop all the nuts and mix with the grated cheese, breadcrumbs and herbs and season with salt and pepper. Mix in the oil to make a soft crumble-type texture. Press into a greased round or deep ovenproof dish and bake for 15 minutes.

To make the vegetable mix, melt butter in a large pan and add the onions. Cook gently for a couple of minutes then add all the chopped vegetables except the courgettes and mushrooms, salt and pepper, grated nutmeg and soy sauce and continue cooking until they are barely tender and still crisp. Add the mushrooms and courgettes, simmer for a further minute, then coat the mixture with flour. Pour in the milk and cook until the sauce thickens (not too runny). Cover the base with the vegetable mixture and cook for 20 minutes. After 10 minutes put on the mixed-together topping ingredients. Serve hot with a salad.

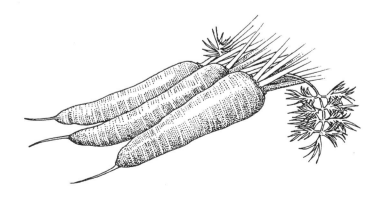

Dips

With all dips, adjust seasoning as necessary

Blue Cheese Dip

75g (3oz) Danish Blue/Stilton
50g (2oz) cream cheese
25g (1oz) Cheddar cheese
15ml (1 tablespoon) mayonnaise

15ml (1 tablespoon) single cream
15ml (1 tablespoon) lemon juice
pinch of salt

Blend all ingredients to a smooth cream and serve with chunks of French bread or raw vegetables.

Avocado Dip

1 medium avocado
30ml (2 tablespoons) single cream
dash of Worcestershire sauce

pinch of cayenne pepper
15ml (1 tablespoon) grated onion
15ml (1 tablespoon) lemon juice

Mash the avocado with the cream to a smooth purée. Add remaining ingredients and mix together. Serve with raw vegetables or cheese biscuits.

75g (3oz) of cream cheese may also be blended with the other ingredients. To stop any discolouration, store with the avocado stone submerged in the dip.

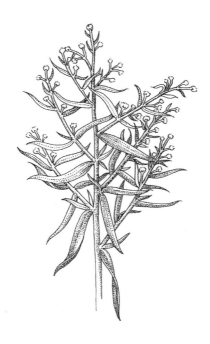

Garlic Dip

2 cloves of garlic, crushed	30 ml (2 tablespoons) single cream
30 ml (2 tablespoons) mayonnaise	salt and pepper

Mix all the ingredients together and serve with raw vegetables.

Tomato Dip

225 g (8 oz) tomatoes	a little tomato purée
1 small onion	pinch of sugar
1 clove of garlic or garlic paste	salt and pepper
15 ml (1 tablespoon) dried marjoram	

Put the tomatoes in hot water, then in cold and peel off the skins. Chop up the flesh, finely chop the onion and combine all the ingredients in a liquidiser or blender and process until you have a thick smooth sauce.

Serve with long stick bread and raw vegetables.

Dhal

225 g (8 oz) lentils (red split lentils, continental green lentils, green or yellow split peas can be used)	5 ml (1 teaspoon) crushed or ground coriander
1 large onion, chopped	5 ml (1 teaspoon) turmeric
30 ml (2 tablespoons) vegetable oil	salt and black pepper
4 ml (1 level teaspoon) mustard seed	30 ml (2 tablespoons) lemon juice, or mix lemon and lime juice together
5 ml (1 teaspoon) crushed or ground cumin	

Soak lentils for 1 hour, drain and add approximately 500 ml (1 pint) of cold water. Bring to the boil and simmer gently for 20–30 minutes until the water is absorbed and the mixture is thick and mushy. Sauté the onion lightly in oil. Add all the spices, except lemon/lime juice, and stir into the onion for a minute or two over a low heat. Take off the heat and stir in the lemon/lime juice with the lentils.

Fresh root ginger, grated and added with lemon/lime juice, adds extra umph!

Oatmeal Soda Bread

450g (1lb) wholemeal flour
115g (4oz) fine oatmeal
7.5ml (1½ teaspoons) cream of tartar

5ml (1 teaspoon) bicarbonate of soda
25g (1oz) butter
400ml (¾ pint) milk/water mix
5ml (1 teaspoon) salt

Preheat oven: 180°C, 350°F; gas mark 4.

Mix together the flour, oatmeal, cream of tartar, bicarbonate of soda, using your fingers, rub in the butter to resemble fine breadcrumbs. Add the milk/water and mix to a soft dough. Turn out the mixture on to a lightly floured surface and knead slightly into a loaf shape or slightly flattened round ball. If you wish, the surface can be deeply scored with a knife in portions. Place on a greased baking sheet and bake in the oven for 30–35 minutes.

Easy and quick to make, delicious to eat straight from the oven or cold with a salad, pasta, croustade or nut roast. Soda bread does not keep well and should be eaten in 1 or 2 days.

Poppy-Seed Cake

115g (4oz) blue poppy-seeds
225 ml (8fl oz) milk
225g (8oz) butter or margarine
225g (8oz) light raw cane sugar

3 eggs separated
225g (8oz) self-raising wholemeal flour

Preheat oven: 180°C, 350°F; gas mark 4.

Grease and line a 20cm (8in) cake tin. Bring the poppy-seeds to the boil in the milk, turn off the heat and leave them to soak for 25 minutes in the covered pan.

Cream the butter and sugar together until light and fluffy. Add the egg yolks, one at a time, and beat thoroughly. Fold the flour gently into the creamed mixture and stir in the seeds and milk. Whisk the egg whites until stiff and carefully incorporate into the mixture. Spoon it into the prepared tin and bake for 1–1¼ hours or until the centre is firm and the cake has stopped 'singing'. Let it stand for 10 minutes, then turn out to cool.

Calke Abbey

Calke Abbey lies deep and secluded in extensive parkland, rich in ancient trees, landscaped by the reclusive Harpur Crewe family, to remain a private, secret place. The house is a Baroque mansion built by Sir John Harpur at the beginning of the eighteenth century. Externally very little alteration has been made since 1841, while inside Calke is the house 'where time has stood still'. Since 1886, when Sir Vauncey Harpur Crewe, the last great collector in a family of passionate collectors, inherited the house practically nothing has changed. Calke presents a unique glimpse of life in a late Victorian household.

Henry Harpur-Crewe, Sir Vauncey's grandson, gave Calke to the National Trust in 1985. With the help of grants from the National Heritage Memorial Fund, English Heritage and a successful appeal, the Trust took on the mammoth task of arresting 60 years of neglect of the house, with its furniture, pictures and extraordinary eclectic collections: toys and dolls, children's clothes, carriages, musical instruments, walking sticks, and, above all, natural history specimens. The Harpur Crewes were fascinated by minerals, fossils, shells, birds' eggs, skeletons and butterflies, and Sir Vauncey, in particular, was an enthusiastic taxidermist; anything that could be stuffed can be found at Calke, some birds and animals shot and stuffed by Sir Vauncey.

A brave decision was taken. Damp, decay and structural weaknesses have been treated, but the contents of Calke have been left much as they were found; pictures are still dark, fabrics faded but beautiful, the decoration of the rooms in the muted colours that time has given them. The house is a splendid clutter of possessions: stuffed heads of longhorn cattle adorn the Entrance Hall; case after case of specimens fill the Saloon, still captioned in Sir Vauncey's spidery hand; late Victorian furniture crowds the Drawing Room; faded maps and worn leatherbound books line the walls of the Library. One item, however, blazes forth in all its original bright colours: the State Bed, given to the family by the Royal Family in the 1730s. Amazingly it remained for 250 years in its original wrappings, never put up because there was no room high enough to accommodate it.

Away from the rooms of state, the drab paint and lime-washed walls give a salutary glimpse into the hard world of the nineteenth-century 'below stairs'. The kitchen and sculleries are particularly grim, with their walls painted blue to keep away the flies, and the stern abjuration to servants 'to waste not, want not' inscribed over the fireplace.

Outdoor staff fared somewhat better; the smithy, tackroom, brew-house and bakehouse are all in elegant eighteenth-century buildings. Today's gardeners can now visit and enjoy the restored vinery, glasshouses, bothy and toolshed, as well as the working kitchen garden where old varieties of fruit and vegetables flourish. Move into the modern age when you need refreshment. The restaurant is a handsome room created from the byre and cattle sheds. The furniture and lighting is modern and underfloor heating cossets twenty-first-century visitors. Local ingredients are important, recipes are imaginative; the superlative mushroom pâté deserves a special mention.

Lentil Soup

225 g (8 oz) red lentils
50 g (2 oz) onion, finely chopped
50 g (2 oz) carrot, grated
1·25 litres (2 pints) vegetable stock

bouquet garni
5 ml (1 teaspoon) tomato purée
salt and pepper

Place the lentils, onion and carrot in a large saucepan and pour in the stock. Add the bouquet garni, tomato purée and bring to the boil. Simmer gently for about 30 minutes until the lentils and vegetables are cooked. Season with salt and pepper and serve with some croûtons.

If you are cholesterol conscious this soup is particularly appropriate as it contains no fat.

Derbyshire Carrot Soup

25 g (1 oz) butter
450 g (1 lb) carrots, grated
1 onion, chopped
1 stick of celery, finely chopped

750 ml (1½ pints) vegetable stock
30 ml (2 tablespoons) milk
2·5 ml (½ teaspoon) sugar
salt and pepper

Melt the butter in a large saucepan and stir in the carrots, onion and celery. Cook for 15 minutes, stirring frequently, over a low heat without allowing the vegetables to colour. Pour in the vegetable stock, bring to the boil and simmer for a further 15 minutes. Add the milk and sugar and season to taste with salt and pepper. Serve with a sprinkling of chopped parsley.

Parsnip and Tomato Bake

115g (4oz) dried pasta shells	250ml (½ pint) milk
2 large parsnips, roughly chopped	5ml (1 teaspoon) English mustard
2 large leeks, roughly chopped	salt and pepper
40g (1½ oz) butter	170g (6oz) Cheddar cheese, grated
25g (1oz) plain flour	3 large tomatoes, sliced

Preheat oven: 180°C, 350°F; gas mark 4.

Cook the pasta according to the instructions on the packet. Cook the chopped parsnips and leeks in boiling water for 10 minutes. Drain and mix them with the cooked pasta.

Make a white sauce by melting the butter, then stirring in and cooking the flour for a few seconds. Gradually add the milk, stirring all the time, until the mixture comes to the boil and a thick sauce is made. Add the mustard and season with salt and pepper. Sprinkle in 140g (5oz) of the grated cheese and heat gently until it has melted into the mixture.

Place half of the vegetable and pasta mixture into an ovenproof casserole dish and layer with slices of tomato covered with half of the sauce. Repeat the layering, then sprinkle the top with the remaining cheese. Bake in the oven for 30 minutes or until the top is golden.

Mushroom Pâté

To fill four–five ramekins

1 small onion, finely chopped	125g (4oz) full-fat cream cheese
140g (5oz) butter	5ml (1 teaspoon) lemon juice
225g (8oz) mushrooms, wiped and chopped	pinch of nutmeg
25g (1oz) fresh white breadcrumbs	salt and freshly ground black pepper

Soften the finely chopped onion in butter and toss the mushrooms for around 30 seconds and cool. Add the breadcrumbs, cheese, lemon juice and seasoning, and turn into the ramekin dishes and chill before serving.

This dish may be served as a first course or as a main meal with salad and crusty bread.

This will keep – even improve – for several days in the fridge.

Sugar-free Banana Cake

75g (3oz) dates	25g (1oz) bran
60ml (2fl oz) water	5ml (1 teaspoon) bicarbonate of
225g (8oz) ripe (or over-ripe)	soda
bananas	50g (2oz) ground almonds
1 egg	2·5ml (½ teaspoon) vanilla essence
75g (3oz) plain wholemeal flour	125ml (5fl oz) low-fat yoghurt

Preheat oven: 180°C, 350°F; gas mark 4.

Grease and flour a 450g (1lb) loaf tin. Place the dates into the water on a low heat until the water is all absorbed. Blend to a smooth paste and then cool. Mash the bananas and whisk the egg and add to the date paste. Lightly fold in the flour, bran, bicarbonate of soda and the ground almonds and gently stir in the vanilla essence and yoghurt. Spoon the mixture into the greased loaf tin and bake for 45 minutes until well risen and just firm. Turn the cake out gently and cool on a wire rack.

Not only is this a wonderfully healthy recipe but an excellent way of using bananas past their best.

Sugar-free Marmalade Scones

140g (5oz) plain wholemeal flour	25g (1oz) margarine
50g (2oz) bran	50g (2oz) sugar-free marmalade
2·5ml (½ teaspoon) bicarbonate	10ml (2 teaspoons) grated orange
of soda	rind
5ml (1 teaspoon) cream of tartar	50ml (2fl oz) skimmed milk

Preheat oven: 230°C, 450°F; gas mark 8.

Mix the flour, bran, bicarbonate of soda and cream of tartar together in a bowl. Rub the margarine into the dry ingredients until the mixture resembles fine breadcrumbs. Gently stir in the marmalade and orange rind and bind with the milk to give a soft dough. Turn out the mixture on to a floured surface and knead lightly before rolling out to approximately 2cm (¾in) thick. Cut out the scones into rounds using a 5cm (2in) cutter and place on a greased baking sheet and bake in the oven for approximately 10 minutes, until brown and well risen. Cool a little on a wire rack.

Try them hot for a special breakfast.

Castle Drogo

Castle Drogo is the last castle built in England, the realisation of a romantic dream for two remarkable men. Julius Drewe founded the Home and Colonial Stores and made a fortune. In 1910, he commissioned Edwin Lutyens to design and build him a great castle. With his son Adrian, he had already chosen the spectacular site. Castle Drogo dominates the Teign Valley in Devon, high up on a spur of Dartmoor, one of the last wildernesses of Britain.

The first sight of this monumental granite pile is breathtaking and yet the building we see now is only one-third of the original design. From the outside Drogo is a true castle, built of huge granite blocks, up to 6 feet thick cut and worked by hand locally. It has turrets, battlements, arrow slits and a portcullis which works with chains and winches. Above the door is the Drogo motto and the Drogo lion.

Inside the castle the atmosphere is more of a grand country house. The walls are hung with family portraits and tapestries, the furniture is comfortable, the rooms well-proportioned but not forbiddingly large. There are many personal mementoes and reminders of the Drewe family, including a touching family memorial room to Adrian, who was killed in the First World War. The tribute was created by his mother.

Lutyens, like his great predecessor, Robert Adam, concerned himself with detail as well as the grand design. He loved kitchens and he designed everything here from the slate shelves, teak draining boards and the vegetable racks by the back door to the wonderful round table under the vaulted roof, complete with special curved chopping boards. Since this dome provided the servants with their only light, it must have felt like washing up in a cathedral.

The grounds are similarly formal and orderly. Huge, beautifully clipped yews frame lawns where by arrangement visitors can play croquet. Refresh yourself after the game or your tour of the castle in the oak-panelled Servants' Hall and Mr Drewe's Study. There are beautiful views over the Teign Valley and waitresses serving good soups, well-cooked puddings and, of course, the ever popular Devon cream teas!

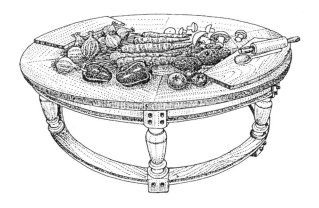

Cream of Watercress Soup

1 medium onion, chopped	500 ml (1 pint) milk
2 small potatoes, chopped	500 ml (1 pint) vegetable stock
50 g (2 oz) butter	salt and pepper
2 bunches of watercress	120 ml (8 tablespoons) double cream

Coarsely chop the onion and potatoes and simmer in a large saucepan with the butter until fairly soft but not browned. Pick over the watercress, discarding any yellow leaves, and add to the pan with the milk and vegetable stock. Bring to the boil and simmer for 20 minutes. Cool a little before liquidising. Pour back into the saucepan and season with salt and pepper. Heat gently just before serving, and with each bowlful swirl in a little cream.

The soup is a lovely colour and healthy too – watercress is an excellent source of iron.

Carrot and Cashew Nut Salad with Yoghurt Dressing

225g (8oz) carrot coarsely grated	115g (4oz) cashew nuts
50g (2oz) raisins	

Dressing

rind and juice of 1 orange	salt and pepper to taste
small pot Greek yoghurt	a little crushed coriander (optional)

Mix salad ingredients together in a bowl. Combine the dressing ingredients and gently stir into the salad. Decorate with chopped coriander or parsley and a twist of orange.

The salad provides a good contrast of creamy, crunchy textures.

Minty Nut Loaf with a Spicy Tomato Topping

225g (8oz) cream cheese	170g (6oz) Brazil nuts, coarsely
115g (4oz) breadcrumbs	chopped
225g (8oz) chopped mushrooms	1 egg
6–8 sprigs mint finely chopped	salt and pepper

Preheat oven: 200°C, 400°F; gas mark 6

* If you do not have a bain-marie, use a roasting tin, but ensure the water comes halfway up the loaf tin.

Lightly grease a 450g (1lb) loaf tin. Mix all the ingredients together in a large bowl and gently press into the greased tin. Cover with a piece of tin foil and bake in a bain-marie* for 45 minutes. Slip a knife around the sides of the tin and turn out on to a warm serving dish.

This dish is best served hot with a salad of your choice.

Spicy Tomato Topping

1 medium onion	pinch of chilli powder
2 cloves of garlic	Worcestershire sauce
30ml (2 tablespoons) oil	Salt and freshly ground black pepper
400g (14oz) tin Italian plum tomatoes	

Chop the onion and garlic and place in a saucepan with the oil and cook over a medium heat until the onion is soft and transparent. Add the tomatoes, chilli powder, a few drops of Worcestershire sauce and seasoning and cook for around 20 minutes, stirring every now and then to break up the tomatoes until the sauce has thickened. Process lightly in a blender or food processor until the sauce is coarsely chopped and still retains some texture.

Vegetable Scramble

115g (4oz) butter
1 small cauliflower broken into florets
4 sticks of celery, chopped
225g (8oz) carrots, sliced
225g (8oz) parsnips diced
450g (1lb) onions, coarsely chopped

400g (14oz) tin chopped tomatoes
herbs of your choice (optional)
225g (8oz) spinach
400g (14oz) tin red kidney beans (drained)
salt and pepper

Melt the butter in a large saucepan and add the first five listed vegetables; sauté gently until barely tender. Pour in the tin of tomatoes and continue to cook for a further 5–10 minutes together with the herbs. In a separate saucepan cook the spinach and when just done add to the other ingredients together with the drained kidney beans. Season and gently heat through.

This dish can either be served on its own or in a large casserole dish, topped with potato and placed under a grill to brown. Decorate with cress.

Queen of Puddings

750ml (1½ pints) milk
225g (8oz) fresh white breadcrumbs
170g (6oz) caster sugar
rind 1 lemon, grated

3 eggs separated
a few fresh strawberries (if available)
13ml (3 level tablespoons) strawberry jam

Preheat oven: 180°C, 350°F; gas mark 4.

Grease generously a 1·25–1·5 litres (2–2½ pint) shallow ovenproof dish. In a saucepan heat the milk to boiling point and remove from the heat. Stir in the breadcrumbs, 50g (2oz) of the caster sugar and the lemon rind. Leave the mixture to soak for around fifteen minutes. Beat the egg yolks into the cooled mixture. Pour it all into the ovenproof dish and bake in a moderate oven for 30 minutes or until the mixture is lightly set. Remove from the oven and cool slightly before placing some fresh strawberries over the top.

In a small saucepan gently melt the jam and pour over the strawberries and filling. Whisk the egg whites until stiff and add the balance of the caster sugar. Continue to whisk until the mixture is stiff and glossy. Spoon or pipe over the top of the pudding and bake for a further 15 minutes until the meringue is lightly browned all over.

With the fresh strawberries this becomes a superlative pudding.

Apricot Bread and Butter Pudding

170g (6oz) dried apricots
75g (3oz) sultanas
450g (1lb) medium-sliced white
 bread, lightly buttered
grated nutmeg or powdered
 cinnamon

225ml (8fl oz) milk
225ml (8fl oz) single cream
170g (6oz) caster sugar
vanilla essence
3 eggs, well beaten
5–10ml (1–2 teaspoons) lemon juice

Preheat oven: 180°C, 350°F; gas mark 4.

Soak the apricots in 500ml (1 pint) water overnight. Generously grease a 1·5 litres (2½ pints) soufflé dish. Soak the sultanas in hot water for 10 minutes, drain and mix with 50g (2oz) apricots. Remove the crusts from the buttered bread and cut into triangles. With the buttered side up, place in the greased soufflé dish and layer with the sultanas and apricots and a sprinkling of nutmeg or cinnamon. In a saucepan heat together the milk, cream and caster sugar to boiling point. Take off the heat and add a few drops of vanilla essence and the well-beaten eggs. Pour the custard over the bread mixture and wait a few minutes for it all to be absorbed. Cover the dish with foil and bake in a bain-marie (see p.44) for 50 minutes or until the pudding is set and firm. Remove from the oven and allow to cool so that it can firm up slightly before turning out on to a serving dish.

To make the sauce, place the remaining apricots and the soaking liquid into a saucepan and simmer for around 15 minutes. Add the balance of the sugar and lemon juice and stir until dissolved. Blend in a liquidiser or food processor and serve separately in a jug.

The apricots add a welcome tang to this traditional pudding.

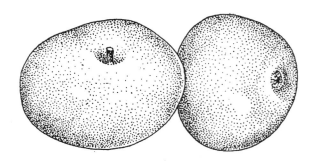

Drogo Carrot Cake

350g (12oz) carrots, grated	225g (8oz) self-raising flour
3 eggs, lightly beaten	2·5ml (½ teaspoon) mixed spice
225g (8oz) soft dark brown sugar	50g (2oz) coconut
125ml (5fl oz) oil	50g (2oz) raisins

Topping for cake

30ml (2 tablespoons) cream cheese	lemon juice to flavour
60ml (4 tablespoons) icing sugar	grated lemon or orange rind

Preheat oven: 150°C, 300°F; gas mark 2.

Grease and line an 18cm (7in) cake tin. In a large mixing bowl combine together all the ingredients until evenly mixed. Spoon into the cake tin and bake for approximately 1¼ hours or until a skewer inserted into the centre comes out clean. Leave to cool in the tin before turning out.

For the topping, beat together the ingredients and spread on top of the cake with a palate knife and decorate with the grated rind.

The coconut, spice and the cream cheese topping give the Drogo Carrot Cake an exotic, tropical flavour.

Devon Cider and Apple Cake

1 large cooking apple, peeled and chopped	225g (8oz) wholemeal or plain flour
50g (2oz) sultanas	5ml (1 teaspoon) baking powder
scant 150ml (¼ pint) dry cider	5ml (1 teaspoon) allspice
115g (4oz) butter	5ml (1 teaspoon) cinnamon
115g (4oz) soft brown sugar	rind 1 lemon, grated
2 eggs, lightly beaten	15ml (1 tablespoon) demerara sugar (optional)

Preheat oven: 180°C, 350°F; gas mark 4.

Grease a 20cm (8in) cake tin. Soak the chopped apple and sultanas in the dry cider. In a separate bowl cream together the butter and sugar until light and fluffy. Gradually beat in, little by little, the eggs. Sift together all the dry ingredients and fold into the mixture together with the lemon rind. Add the soaked fruit and cider and gently mix until it is well incorporated. Spoon into the prepared tin, scatter the demerara sugar over the top and bake for 45–60 minutes.

Charlecote Park

The Lucy family have lived at Charlecote since the twelfth century, though Sir Thomas Lucy built the present house in 1551. The mellow brick exterior, faded to a delicate rose pink, seems totally Elizabethan but in fact only the Gatehouse is unaltered and authentic – generations of Lucys have made their changes over the succeeding centuries. Legend has it that the youthful William Shakespeare was caught poaching deer in the park. Sir Thomas, the resident magistrate, fined him and ordered him to be flogged. Fleeing to London to find fame and fortune, Shakespeare immortalised Sir Thomas as the fussy, vainglorious Mr Justice Shallow in *Henry IV Part II* and *The Merry Wives of Windsor*. Deer still roam the park.

By the time George Hammond Lucy inherited in 1823, the estate had become shabby and run down. He married a young Welsh heiress, Mary Elizabeth, and the couple enthusiastically set about restoring the property and redecorating the interior. The result is fascinating; the rooms are rich and to our eyes wonderfully Victorian, but George and Mary Elizabeth saw them as Elizabethan. The Dining Room and the Library, added by George, have heavily ornamented, plastered ceilings, carved oak panelling and richly coloured wallpapers. Some furniture was made specially in Elizabethan style, while seventeenth-century ebony seat furniture – bought because the Lucys thought they had belonged to Elizabeth I – have tapestry seats and backs worked by Mary Elizabeth. The

Great Hall, resplendent with family portraits, was also transformed by George Hammond Lucy: its barrel-vaulted ceiling looks like wood but is painted plaster, and so are the stonework walls; even the Elizabethan fireplace is Victorian.

As young bride, mother, widow and grandmother, Mary Elizabeth lived for 60 years in the house and loved every nook and cranny. You can see her Drawing Room decorated in amber silk and furnished with delicate, rather uncomfortable furniture. Her beloved little harp is still sitting in one corner. Above the tackroom in the stables there is an interesting video using excerpts from her diary to bring alive Victorian Charlecote.

When I visited, a local school was learning about spit-roasting in the kitchen. The cool brew-house is full of old machinery and enormous wooden vats. In the stables are the Lucy coaches and the saddles, bridles and coachmen's uniforms.

In the garden, alongside a huge herbaceous border is a delightful thatched summer-house. Mary Elizabeth furnished it with child-sized furniture and objects for the amusement of her children. Nearby is the Victorian Orangery now used as the restaurant; feathery green plants, terracotta walls, blue chairs and rush matting give a conservatory atmosphere. Herbs from the garden add a fresh taste to the crisp salads, sustaining soups and wholesome hot dishes. Warwickshire apples are famous – light and moist Charlecote Apple Cake is a recipe worthy of them.

Tarragon and Vegetable Soup

1 medium onion	10 ml (1 dessertspoon) tomato purée
1 large potato	400 g (14 oz) tin tomatoes
1 medium parsnip	10 ml (1 dessertspoon) tarragon
1 green pepper	(preferably fresh)
1 stick of celery	500 ml (1 pint) vegetable stock
1 large carrot	salt and pepper
50 g (2 oz) butter	150 ml (¼ pint) single cream

Prepare all the vegetables and chop coarsely. Sweat in a large saucepan with the butter until slightly softened. Add the tomato purée, tin of tomatoes, tarragon and enough vegetable stock to cover. Bring to the boil and simmer until all the vegetables are very soft. Process in a liquidiser, return to the pan and reheat. Adjust the seasoning and stir in the single cream before serving.

Tarragon has a delicate yet distinctive flavour.

Grape, Mushroom and Peanut Salad

115g (4oz) mushrooms, sliced
50g (2oz) dry roasted peanuts
225g (8oz) black grapes, halved and
   de-seeded

thin coating of French dressing
parsley, finely chopped to decorate

Combine the first three ingredients, pour over the French dressing and gently turn the salad with a wooden spoon. Decorate with the parsley and serve.

This salad is unusual, nourishing and tasty.

Pinenut and Spinach Jalousie

675g (1½lb) puff pastry

Stuffing
1 beaten egg (use only half and save
   balance to glaze the jalousie)
75g (3oz) fresh brown breadcrumbs
juice and rind of half a lemon

pinch of oregano
pinch of sage
fresh parsley, chopped

Filling
1 small onion, chopped
50g (2oz) pinenuts
50g (2oz) hazelnuts, chopped

50g (2oz) white breadcrumbs
1 beaten egg
pinch of nutmeg

Spinach Mixture
225g (8oz) spinach, cooked and
   well drained
115g (4oz) Cambazola cheese (or
   other soft, blue cheese)

pinch of nutmeg
freshly ground pepper

Preheat oven: 220°C, 425°F; gas mark 7.

Combine the ingredients of the stuffing and the spinach mixture in two separate bowls. For the filling, sauté the onion and mix with the other ingredients. Roll out the pastry into two large rectangles and place one on a greased baking sheet. Leaving a margin round the edge, spread with the stuffing, then the filling and lastly the spinach mixture. Brush the edge with a little beaten egg and place the second rectangle on top, sealing the edges well. Make horizontal cuts in the top pastry from one side to the other, 3·75cm (1½in) apart. Brush with the remaining beaten egg and bake for 30–45 minutes until golden brown.

Broccoli and Pasta Bake

Serves eight

225g (8oz) dry pasta shells
225g (8oz) broccoli florets
1·75 litres (3 pints) milk
1 large onion, peeled
4 bay leaves
grated nutmeg

12 peppercorns
75g (3oz) butter
75g (3oz) flour
350g (12oz) cheese, grated
salt and pepper

Preheat oven: 200°C, 400°F; gas mark 6.

Cook and drain the pasta shells according to instructions on the packet. Lightly cook the broccoli until just tender, drain and roughly chop. In a saucepan bring the milk to the boil with the onion, bay leaves, grated nutmeg and peppercorns, then cover and leave to cool before straining.

Make a cheese sauce by melting the butter, stir in the flour and cook for 2–3 minutes. Gradually pour in the strained milk and bring to the boil, stirring constantly until the sauce thickens. Take off the heat and add 300g (10oz) grated cheese and season with salt and pepper.

Combine the pasta shells, broccoli and cheese sauce together and spoon into an ovenproof dish. Sprinkle on the balance of the cheese and bake in the oven for about 20 minutes or until golden and bubbling.

Serve with a tomato or green salad.

Bread and Butter Pudding

8 slices of white bread, buttered
30ml (2 tablespoons) demerara sugar
115g (4oz) sultanas

4 eggs
675ml (1¼ pints) milk
ground nutmeg

Preheat oven: 180°C, 350°F; gas mark 4.

Grease a 1·25–1·5 litres (2–2½ pint) ovenproof dish. Cut the bread and butter slices in half and arrange, buttered side up, in layers in the ovenproof dish, sprinkling the layers with the sugar and sultanas. Finish with a layer of bread and sugar. Whisk the eggs lightly and add to the milk. Pour the whole lot over the bread, sprinkle some freshly grated nutmeg on top and bake in the oven for 30–40 minutes until set and lightly brown. Serve warm.

Crispy Crumble Fruit Pie

225g (8oz) brown flour	1 egg
225g (8oz) porridge oats	little water
115g (4oz) butter	675g (1½lb) cooked fruits
225g (8oz) light brown sugar	

Preheat oven: 180°C, 350°F; gas mark 4.

Suggested fruits are apple, blackberries, rhubarb, gooseberries, plums, etc., simmered with a scant amount of water and sugar to taste until barely tender. A little cinnamon would go particularly well with apples and plums as would ground ginger with rhubarb.

In a mixing bowl place the flour and porridge oats, then add the butter and rub in lightly using your finger tips. When it all looks crumbly and the fat evenly dispersed, add the sugar and combine well. Mix the egg with half of this mixture, together with a little water, to form a dough. Press into the base and sides of a 1·75 litre (3 pint) pie dish. Fill with the cooked fruit of your choice and sprinkle on the balance of the crumble. Bake in the oven for 30–40 minutes until the topping is tinged with brown.

Date, Orange and Cinnamon Flapjack Pudding

225g (8oz) dates, chopped	30ml (2 tablespoons) syrup
orange juice	225g (8oz) porridge oats
pinch of cinnamon	115g (4oz) soft, light brown sugar
170g (6oz) butter	115g (4oz) plain wholemeal flour

Preheat oven: 190°C, 375°F; gas mark 5.

Grease an 18×18cm (7×7in) tin. In a saucepan cook the dates with enough orange juice to make a spreading consistency together with a pinch of cinnamon. Melt together the butter and syrup and combine together with all the dry ingredients. Press half this mixture into the greased tin, spread over the dates and cover with the remaining mixture. Bake in the oven for 20–25 minutes until just browning.

Serve cold in slices or warm as a pudding with some cream.

Charlecote Apple Cake

450g (1 lb) self-raising flour
2·5ml (½ teaspoon) mixed spices
2·5ml (½ teaspoon) nutmeg
pinch of salt
170g (6oz) sultanas
170g (6oz) firm green apples, finely chopped

225g (8oz) soft margarine
225g (8oz) caster sugar
2 eggs
150ml (¼ pint) milk
1 firm green apple, sliced
15ml (1 tablespoon) demerara sugar

Preheat oven: 180°C, 350°F; gas mark 4.

Grease and line a 23cm (9in) cake tin; Sift together the flour, spices and salt and stir in the sultanas and chopped apples. In a large mixing bowl cream together the soft margarine and caster sugar until light and fluffy. Gradually beat in the eggs (don't worry if the mixture should curdle slightly). Gently stir in the flour, spices and fruit and pour in the milk to make a stiffish mixture. Spoon into the cake tin and smooth out the top. Brush the top with water and lay the apple slices in a circle. Brush once again with water and sprinkle on the demerara sugar. Bake in the oven for approximately 1¼ hours. Cool slightly before turning out on to a wire rack.

Scurvy

Scurvy has long been recognised as an affliction of the poor and sailors deprived of fresh food on long voyages (see p.28). But now it has been argued by Susan Maclean Kybett, Fellow of the Royal Historical Society, that the highest and mightiest in the land were similarly afflicted. Henry VIII, his daughters Mary and Elizabeth, and his colossally wealthy prelate, Cardinal Wolsey, all manifested symptoms of scurvy. Meat formed the mainstay of a privileged diet, while fresh fruit and vegetables were regarded as more suitable for peasants. One prominent physician warned that fruit 'do ingender ylle humours and be ofteytimes the cause of putrified fevers'. If the King suffered from dietary malnutrition, then it is more than probable that most of his courtiers did too.

Chirk Castle

On the borders, 'the Marches' between England and Wales, Edward I organised a chain of castles to be built to consolidate his conquests against the Welsh. Chirk Castle was begun in 1295 by Roger Mortimer, on land confiscated from Llywelyn ap Gruffydd ap Madog – 'the dragon of Chirk with the obstinate spear'. As visitors approach through immense wrought-iron gates, up a long drive and then climb a steep hill under the huge, stone-block walls and drum towers of the forbidding entrance, it is not difficult to imagine the turbulent medieval history of Chirk. Many of its owners were powerful political figures and most of them met untimely ends.

Although life at Chirk is now more tranquil, on each side of the great internal courtyard you can taste the lives of previous inhabitants of the castle. Adam's Tower is medieval: below the guardroom is a damp, evocatively nasty dungeon; above is a series of small rooms equipped with accurately placed 'murder holes' in the floors. The Magistrates' Court is a narrow chamber with a charming rough-cut frieze, the only plasterwork to survive the Civil War. Chirk, then owned by Sir Thomas Myddelton, was besieged and sacked during the war, but the family returned to restore the castle, and their descendants live here still.

The castle proper is entered on the north side. The Cromwell Hall feels seventeenth century but was in fact created by the Victorian architect A. W. Pugin. A graceful staircase leads up to the eighteenth-century state rooms – the State Dining Room, Saloon, Drawing Room and a 100-foot Long Gallery, sumptuously furnished and hung with portraits by Kneller, Lely, Van Dyck and others.

On the south side of the quadrangle is the Servants' Hall, dark but not depressing; servants ate here and a strict hierarchy determined who sat near the fire, who by the door and who was served first. On the walls are lively pictures of, amongst others, 'Welch Wilkes, Chirk Castle scullion' and a set of severe rules – 'No noise, no strife nor swear at all, But all be decent in the Hall.'

Good guidelines for today's visitors to observe in the tea-room in the delightful Old Kitchen opposite, where the tables in the area for booked parties are in circular turrets, with wonderful views. Here are interesting soups, good savoury tarts, a vegetable crumble that is a main-course variation on an old favourite.

Notes to servants that hang in the Servants' Hall
at Chirk Castle:

Servants' Hall
No noise, no strife nor swear at all
But all be decent in the Hall.

Rules to be Observed
That every servant must:

Take off his hat on entering here
Sit in proper place at table
Keep himself clean becoming his station
Shut the door after him
Drink in his turn

That no servant be:

Guilty of cursing or swearing
Telling tales
Speaking disrespectfully of anyone
Wasting meat or drink
Intermeddling with any other's business unless requested to assist

NB The person offending to be deprived his allowance of beer – for the first offence three days, second offence one whole month and more often his behaviour to be laid before Mr Myddelton.

Cauliflower Soup

50g (2oz) butter
1 large onion, chopped
900g (2lb) cauliflower, chopped
1 large potato, chopped
1 litre (1¾ pints) vegetable stock

salt and freshly ground black pepper
250ml (½ pint) double cream
generous amount of parsley,
 chopped

In a large saucepan melt the butter and gently fry the chopped onion until transparent. Add the cauliflower, potato and vegetable stock, bring to the boil and simmer with a lid on for around 20 minutes or until the vegetables are tender. Take off the heat and cool slightly before blending in a food processor. Return to the pan and season with salt and pepper. Before serving pour in the double cream and garnish with chopped fresh parsley.

This recipe can be used to make celery or leek soup, in place of the cauliflower.

Leek Pie

Pastry
115g (4oz) wholemeal flour
50g (2oz) plain flour
75g (3oz) Cheddar cheese,
 grated

75g (3oz) butter or margarine,
 chilled
1 egg yolk
cold water to mix

Filling
115g (4oz) butter or margarine
900g (2lb) leeks (sliced 1·25cm
 [½in] rounds)
115g (4oz) flour
400ml (¾ pint) milk

rind and juice ½ lemon
pinch of ground nutmeg
50g (2oz) chopped hazelnuts
50g (2oz) raisins
salt and pepper

Preheat oven: 200°C, 400°F; gas mark 6.

Place the flours and grated cheese in a food processor together with the chilled butter and process for a few seconds until the mixture resembles coarse breadcrumbs. Take off the lid and add the egg yolk together with 15ml (1 tablespoon) of cold water. Process until the mixture forms a ball around the central column. If this does not happen after a few seconds, take off the lid and add a little more water. Place in a plastic bag and leave to rest in the fridge while you make the filling.

Melt the butter in a large saucepan and sauté the chopped leeks gently until tender. Stir in the flour and cook over a gentle heat for 2 or 3 minutes. Pour in the milk and bring to the boil, stirring all the time with a wooden spoon, until the sauce has thickened. Add all the remaining ingredients and season to taste. Place in an oven-proof pie dish. Roll out the pastry, cover the pie and brush with milk or beaten egg. Place in the oven and bake for 30 minutes.

This pie has a particularly tasty filling.

Vegetable Crumble

Crumble Topping
115 g (4 oz) butter
170 g (6 oz) wholemeal flour

170 g (6 oz) mature Cheddar cheese, grated
50 g (2 oz) chopped walnuts

Vegetable Base
800 g (1 lb 12 oz) mixed vegetables – such as potatoes, carrots, parsnips, leeks and mushrooms
1 large onion, chopped
50 g (2 oz) butter
25 g (1 oz) wholemeal flour

small tin chopped tomatoes
150 ml (¼ pint) vegetable stock
250 ml (½ pint) milk
a good handful of chopped parsley
salt and freshly ground black pepper

Preheat oven: 190°C, 375°F; gas mark 5.

Rub the butter into the flour until the mixture resembles fine crumbs. Add the cheese, nuts and some black pepper to taste and combine well.

Chop all the vegetables and in a large saucepan melt the butter and sauté the onion until transparent. Add the prepared vegetables and cook over a gentle heat, stirring occasionally, for 10–15 minutes. Take off the heat, stir in the flour and the remaining ingredients. Bring to the boil and simmer for 15–20 minutes until the vegetables are just tender. Transfer to a large ovenproof dish and press the crumble topping over the vegetables. Bake in the oven for 30–40 minutes. Garnish with a little parsley.

Country Cheese Tart with Garlic and Fresh Herbs

Pastry

115g (4oz) plain wholewheat flour
50g (2oz) self-raising flour
pinch of salt

50g (2oz) margarine
50g (2oz) vegetarian lard
cold water

Filling

25g (1oz) butter
50g (2oz) onion, finely chopped
2 cloves garlic, chopped
3 eggs, lightly beaten
150ml (¼ pint) milk
150ml (¼ pint) double cream

freshly chopped herbs of your choice
75g (3oz) mature Welsh Cheddar cheese
salt and pepper
2 tomatoes, chopped
parsley, chopped

Preheat oven: 200°C, 400°F; gas mark 6.

Place the flours and salt in a mixing bowl, then cut the fats into small cubes and add to the bowl. Using your fingertips, gently rub the fat into the flour. When the mixture looks crumbly start to sprinkle in around 30ml (2 tablespoons) of water. Gradually work this in with a knife, then draw together to form a ball with your hands. Place the pastry in a polythene bag and refrigerate for 20 minutes.

Roll out the pastry and line a 20cm (8in) flan tin. Melt the butter in a saucepan and gently sauté the chopped onion and garlic until lightly brown. Cool for a few minutes before spreading over the pastry case. Place the eggs, milk, cream, herbs and Cheddar cheese in a bowl, beat until well mixed and season with salt and pepper. Pour the mixture over the onions and sprinkle with chopped tomatoes and fresh parsley. Place the flan on a baking sheet in the oven and bake for 30–40 minutes until golden brown (reduce heat to a medium oven, and cook for a further 5–10 minutes if the egg mixture is not quite set).

Stilton and Celery Tart (an alternative filling)

As for Country Cheese Tart but substitute 75g (3oz) of blue Stilton cheese for the 75g (3oz) mature Welsh Cheddar and add 225g (8oz) very thinly sliced celery, simmered in a little butter until tender and then drained (omit the herbs, garlic and tomatoes).

Lemon Tart

Pastry

115g (¼lb) plain flour	50g (2oz) icing sugar
medium pinch of salt	1 egg yolk
50g (2oz) butter	1 tablespoon water

Filling

225g (8oz) caster sugar	4 eggs, lightly beaten
225g (8oz) butter	2 lemons – juice and grated rind

Preheat oven: 180°C, 350°F; gas mark 4.

Combine flour, salt, butter and sugar in a food processor and process until the mixture resembles coarse breadcrumbs. Add the egg yolk and the tablespoons of water. Process until the mixture forms a ball. Do not overprocess – stop the machine as soon as the ball has formed. Place the pastry in a plastic bag and rest it in the fridge while you make the filling.

In a saucepan melt together the caster sugar and butter. Take off the heat, stir in the lightly beaten eggs, then the juice and rind of the lemons. Roll out the pastry and line a 23cm (9in) loose bottomed flan tin. Prick the base with a fork. Pour the mixture into the pastry case and place the flan tin in the oven on a baking sheet (this will ensure that the base is firm and that the filling sets well). Bake for 30 minutes when the top should be a light golden brown.

The pastry recipe above is new to this edition. This lemon tart has become a great favourite with fellow cooks who, like all enthusiasts, try to hone the recipe to perfection. A young friend, inspired by another more famous cook, Jamie Oliver, has worked on his original pastry recipe. In her own words she's 'tweaked' it a little and now, with its wonderful Chirk lemon filling, we both think it's the best lemon tart in the world.

Claremont
Landscape Garden

Space today is a luxury to be cherished, particularly in the built-up south-east of England. Claremont – 20 hectares, (50 acres) of spacious eighteenth-century landscape garden – is bounded on one side by the busy A307, the old trunk road from London to Portsmouth, and on all the other sides by the houses and gardens of prosperous suburbia.

The landscape garden is a distinctly English contribution to the history of gardening – a reaction to the earlier, formal planning and planting. In landscape gardens, park and garden merge imperceptibly into a harmonious whole, nature is respected and enhanced rather than rigidly moulded to a pattern. Flowers play a minor role; water, trees, and antique buildings are more important.

At Claremont, all these pleasures can be experienced; the reflection of trees on water, the impressive amphitheatre, a ruined grotto for melancholy thoughts, an elegant island pavilion. Black swans and myriad duck float on the lake which also contains huge slow-moving carp.

This garden, so peaceful now, has had a chequered history. Many owners and gardeners have altered and influenced Claremont, amongst them Sir John Vanbrugh, Charles Bridgeman, William Kent, Lancelot 'Capability' Brown, Lord Clive of India and Prince Leopold of Saxe-Coburg, Queen Victoria's uncle. By 1976 the garden was a 'lake within a wood', the grotto decayed, the amphitheatre invisible and the original planting obscured beneath self-sown birch and scrub. Restoration meant stripping back layers of undergrowth to reveal the lovely garden we enjoy today, not one man's creation but the essence of the English Landscape Garden, art and nature combined to form a succession of contrasts for the onlooker's pleasure.

A right turn at the entrance to the garden takes one to the tea-room, built in a rustic style of which William Kent would have approved. Peacocks scratch outside. Inside, now, you will find good, simple home-made fare. The menu changes according to the person in charge. The recipes here were given to me by a previous chef who researched and adapted recipes of the eighteenth century and invented others which provide a delicate compliment to one of Claremont's famous owners, Clive of India. He has now moved on but his ideas, which are both imaginative and delicious, a rich legacy to Claremont, are too good to leave out.

Spring Soup

1 large onion	1 bunch of nettle tops
2 sticks of celery	1 bunch of watercress
2 carrots	1 bunch of dandelion leaves
2 tomatoes	450g (1 lb) spinach or sorrel
1 bayleaf	salt and pepper
pinch of thyme	thick cream to serve
2·5 litres (4 pints) water	

Sauté in a large pan with a little butter or oil the chopped onion, celery, carrots, tomatoes, bayleaf and thyme. When softened add the water, bring to the boil and simmer for half an hour. Strain the stock (or if you would like a more substantial soup, leave the stock ingredients) and add all the leaf mixtures. Reheat and as soon as they have turned dark green and wilted, liquidise in a blender or processor. Heat before serving and add some thick cream.

This must be made early in the year before young growth becomes tough and woody.

Salamongundy

More of a concept than a recipe – in 1747 Mrs Hannah Glasse wrote, 'you may always make Salamongundy of such things as you have, according to your fancy'.

Salamongundy is basically an English composite salad, similar to the Mediterranean Salade Niçoise. Originally it consisted of cold meats combined with lettuce, grapes and anchovies but there are many variations.

In this vegetarian version the base consists of a mixture of colourful and tasty leaves such as curly endive, cos, lollo rosso, oakleaf, young dandelion leaves, spinach – whatever is available. A layer is placed on a large flat dish, then other vegetables are layered or piled on top to make a colourful display. You can use leeks and mushrooms cooked 'à la grecque' in a little vinegar and olive oil and cooled; tiny new potatoes cooked and dressed with walnut oil and mint; raw carrot with a poppy-seed dressing; blanched green beans, chopped tomatoes, etc. Hard-boiled eggs can also be added and there should always be a fruit element such as chopped red apples or grapes.

Place the dish in the centre of the table and let your guests help themselves. Served with a good selection of bread and a bottle of Alsace Gewurztraminer, Salamongundy makes a perfect summer lunch or supper.

Rice and Chickpea Flour Pancakes with an Indian Spice Stuffing

Pancakes

50g (2oz) besan flour (Gram flour) – available from Indian foodstores or health food shops
50g (2oz) ground rice

approximately 225ml (8fl oz) milk
1 egg, lightly beaten
salt and pepper

Filling

1 large onion
30ml (2 tablespoons) oil
5ml (1 teaspoon) whole cumin
5ml (1 teaspoon) kalonji (onion seeds or nigella)

10ml (2 teaspoons) Madras curry paste
900g (2lb) waxy potatoes
400g (14oz) tin tomatoes
50g (2oz) frozen peas
salt and pepper

Sift the besan flour into a bowl. Add the ground rice and mix to a paste with a little of the milk. Mix in the beaten egg and the balance of the milk to make a pouring batter. Season and allow to rest for approximately 20 minutes.

Fry the pancakes in a non-stick frying pan or with the addition of a little oil and, as each one is done, stack on a plate and keep covered in a low oven.

To make the filling, fry the chopped onion in oil, add cumin and kalonji and continue to sauté for a few minutes. Mix in the curry paste and potatoes which have been peeled and cut into approximately 2·5cm (1in) cubes. Pour in the tin of tomatoes and add a little water, if necessary, to cover. Put on a lid and simmer until the potatoes are done (but still firm). Raise the heat and cook uncovered until the sauce is thick, stirring frequently. Add the frozen peas and salt and pepper to taste.

Place an equal amount of filling on each pancake and roll up. Serve with a coconut relish made by soaking desiccated coconut in milk for an hour, draining and then adding chopped cucumbers and fresh parsley or coriander or natural yoghurt with the addition of some freshly chopped mint.

Tomato and Basil Tart with Olive Oil Pastry

Pastry
1 clove of garlic, crushed
75ml (5 tablespoons) olive oil
15ml (1 tablespoon) water

170g (6oz) plain flour
1 teaspoon (5ml) salt

Filling
1 large onion
45ml (3 tablespoons) olive oil
1·4kg (3lb) tomatoes

1 bunch of fresh basil, chopped
5ml (1 teaspoon) sugar
salt and pepper

Preheat oven: 200°C, 400°F; gas mark 6.

Fry the garlic in oil and allow to cool a little before adding the water (the oil will spit if too hot). Beat into the flour and salt and form the mixture into a ball. It is not possible to roll this pastry in the traditional way. However, it can either be rolled between two sheets of greaseproof paper or pressed into a 20cm (8in) loose-bottomed flan tin, using fingertips. Chill for approximately 20 minutes. Bake blind in the oven for 15–20 minutes. Lower oven heat to: 180°C, 350°F; gas mark 4.

To make the filling, chop the onion finely and sauté in the oil for a minute or two. Skin and de-seed the tomatoes, place in the pan and cook until reduced to a thick pulp. Add half of the basil, sugar and salt and pepper to taste and spoon into the baked flan case. Bake in a low oven for about half an hour. Just before serving sprinkle with the remaining basil and serve with a green salad and crusty bread.

Apple and Stilton Strudel

1 large packet strudel pastry (filo pastry)	5 Granny Smith apples
60 ml (4 tablespoons) vegetable oil	115 g (4 oz) fresh white bread-crumbs
450 g (1 lb) Stilton cheese	30 ml (2 tablespoons) melted butter

Preheat oven: 200°C, 400°F; gas mark 6.

Defrost the packet of strudel pastry and lay out five rectangular sheets with the short edge nearest you. Brush each sheet with vegetable oil before laying on the next. Crumble the Stilton over the pastry, leaving a small gap at either end and at the sides. Peel and chop the apples and cut into chunks. Spread on top of the cheese and sprinkle over a good handful of fresh breadcrumbs. Starting at the edge nearest you, roll up the strudel as tightly as possible without breaking the pastry. Place on a greased baking sheet with the edges down. Brush with melted butter and sprinkle on the balance of the breadcrumbs. Bake in the oven for approximately 30 minutes.

Cut into large slices and serve as a lunch or supper dish with a salad of your choice.

Carrot Halwa

675 g (1½ lb) carrots, peeled and finely grated	170 g (6 oz) caster sugar
115 g (4 oz) unsalted butter	50 g (2 oz) ground almonds
6 cardamon pods	30 ml (2 tablespoons) honey
50 g (2 oz) sultanas	400 g (14 oz) can condensed milk
	a few drops of almond essence

Cover the grated carrots with water and cook gently until soft. Drain well and return the carrots to the saucepan, then add all the other ingredients and cook gently until the mixture is quite thick. Press the mixture into a baking tray so that it is about 3·75 cm (1½ in) in depth. Cool and then refrigerate until required. Serve with single cream in small squares as a pudding.

This pudding is extremely rich and has a subtle, delicate flavour.

Cliveden

High up above the Thames in Buckinghamshire stands Cliveden, an Italianate villa built in the mid-nineteenth century. It is the third house to have been built on the site, the first two having been destroyed by fire. The present house was built in 1850–1 to the design of Sir Charles Barry for the 2nd Duke of Sutherland. It was during the early years of the nineteenth century, when the first house was a ruin, that the great statesman George Canning is thought to have spent hours beneath the oak tree that now bears his name. The view of the Thames from beneath its branches is one of the most famous on the river.

The house is now used as an hotel, but the visitor can stand on the immense south-facing terrace, look down over the Borghese balustrade and across the clipped conical yews and geometrically planted beds of the parterre to the river far below and the rolling hills beyond. The 1st Lord Astor, who bought the house in 1893, laid out the Long Garden and the delightful water garden with its irregular ponds, carp, stepping stones and a pagoda. He filled the grounds with statuary, including Roman marble sarcophagi, and built the huge Fountain of Love to the north of the house.

When his eldest son, Waldorf, married the Virginian beauty Nancy Langhorne in 1906, Lord Astor gave them the house. As Lady Astor, Nancy became the first female Member of Parliament to take her seat, and between the wars she made Cliveden a centre of political and literary society. A woman of strongly held views, she detested the consumption of alcohol and enjoyed several famous verbal duels with Sir Winston Churchill on the subject. She was also a firm Christian Scientist, and although she herself enjoyed good health, her opposition to orthodox medical treatment could bring problems to her friends and family.

After a walk in the grounds at Cliveden, visit the National Trust Restaurant in the white painted conservatory on the east side of the house. Vegetarian food has been excellent here for many years. Some of the recipes were given to me by Maureen Smith who has now retired. Julie Cullen continues the tradition and I am delighted to include some of her delicious ideas. Her Carrot, Courgette and Caraway Cake not only tastes good but looks wonderful. I've never encountered a cake speckled in orange and green before.

Lentil and Wine Pâté

350g (12oz) red lentils	2 cloves of garlic, crushed
750ml (1½ pints) red wine	10ml (2 teaspoons) dried herbs
50g (2oz) butter	125g (4oz) ground mixed nuts
2 large onions, chopped	125g (4oz) cheese, grated
125g (4oz) carrots, finely chopped	2 eggs, lightly beaten
2 sticks celery, finely chopped	salt and pepper

Preheat oven: 180°C, 350°F; gas mark 4.

Prepare a 900g (2lb) loaf tin by lining the base and sides with silicon paper. Place the lentils and red wine in a saucepan, bring to the boil and simmer for 20 minutes until the lentils are tender and the liquid absorbed. In a large saucepan melt the butter and fry the onions, carrot, celery and garlic for approximately 10 minutes when they should be softened and light brown. Take off the heat and add the cooked lentils, herbs, nuts, cheese and eggs. Mix everything together and season with salt and pepper. Spoon the mixture into the prepared tin and cover with a piece of foil. Bake in the oven for around 1¼ hours, removing the foil for the last 15 minutes. Allow to rest for a while to firm up the pâté before very carefully turning out and removing the lining paper.

This pâté can be served either hot or cold, decorated with fresh herbs and accompanied by fresh crusty bread.

Cheese and Lentil Pâté

450g (1 lb) red lentils
25g (1 oz) butter
2 large onions, finely chopped
1 clove of garlic, crushed

225g (8oz) cheese, grated
handful chopped fresh parsley
4 eggs, lightly beaten
salt and pepper

Preheat oven: 180°C, 350°F; gas mark 4.

Prepare a 900g (2lb) loaf tin by lining the base and sides with silicon paper. In a large saucepan place the lentils with just enough water to cover. Bring to the boil and simmer until the lentils are cooked and have absorbed all the water. This will take around 20 minutes. While they are cooking melt the butter in a small frying pan and gently sauté the finely chopped onions and crushed garlic until transparent. Add to the cooked lentils together with the grated cheese, parsley and eggs. Season well with salt and pepper and spoon into the loaf tin. Bake in the oven for 1¼ hours. Leave to cool before turning out and removing the lining paper.

Serve this pâté cold with a salad.

Butter Bean Pâté

Makes four–six ramekins

225g (8oz) dried butter beans
2 cloves of garlic, crushed
juice ½ lemon
150ml (¼ pint) double cream

salt and freshly ground black pepper
freshly chopped parsley
15ml (1 tablespoon) spring onions,
    finely chopped

Soak the beans overnight, drain and cook in fresh water until they are very tender. Drain and allow to cool. Place the beans in a food processor together with the garlic, lemon juice and double cream and process until the mixture is almost smooth (if you wish you can also have a more coarse texture). Season with salt and pepper and stir in the parsley and chopped spring onions. Pack into individual ramekins and chill until required (it will keep well in a fridge).

Serve with crispy bread. Makes an excellent starter or serve with salads as a light main course.

Leek and Mushroom Croustade

Base
75g (3oz) fresh breadcrumbs
115g (4oz) mixed chopped nuts
5ml (1 teaspoon) dried mixed herbs
  (or fresh if you have them)
50g (2oz) butter
salt and pepper

Topping
50g (2oz) butter
1 large onion, chopped
15ml (1 tablespoon) flour
250–400ml (½–¾ pint) milk
170g (6oz) cheese, grated
350g (12oz) leeks, cooked and
  sliced
225g (8oz) mushrooms, slightly
  cooked
salt and pepper

Preheat oven: 180°C, 350°F; gas mark 4.

Mix together all the ingredients for the base, season well with salt and pepper and press into the base of a 20cm (8in) loose-bottomed flan tin. Bake in the oven for 15 minutes until golden brown.

Melt the butter in a saucepan and fry the onion until transparent. Stir in the flour and cook for a minute or two before pouring in the milk. Stirring all the time, bring to the boil, then add 115g (4oz) of the grated cheese, cooked leeks and mushrooms. Season with salt and pepper and spoon on top of the croustade. Sprinkle on the balance of the cheese and return the croustade to the oven and bake for around 20 minutes. Leave to cool slightly to give the mixture time to set before taking out of the tin.

Tastes good both lukewarm and cold!

Apple Chutney

1 onion, chopped
1·35kg (3lb) apples peeled, cored
  and roughly chopped, any variety
  will do
225g (8oz) sultanas
1 teaspoon ground ginger
1 teaspoon mixed spice
300ml (10fl oz) malt vinegar
225g (8oz) granulated sugar

Place all the ingredients, other than the sugar, in a large saucepan, bring to the boil and simmer until the mixture is soft and pulpy. Add the sugar and stir until dissolved. You can pot the mixture hot or cold.

This chutney is delicious with cheese and is a great way to deal with a glut of apples.

Butter Bean and Leek Bake

170g (6oz) dried butter beans	2 large onions, chopped
250ml (½ pint) milk	2 cloves of garlic, crushed
3 leeks, sliced and cooked	25g (1oz) flour
50g (2oz) butter	freshly chopped parsley

Topping

50g (2oz) breadcrumbs	Salt and pepper
50g (2oz) cheese, grated	

Preheat oven: 190°C, 375°F; gas mark 5.

Soak and cook the butter beans in water until soft. Drain and reserve their liquid. Make their liquid up to 400ml (¾ pint) with the milk. Cook the leeks in a little boiling water until tender and drain well. Melt the butter in a saucepan and gently sauté the onion and garlic until transparent. Stir in the flour and cook for a further minute or two before adding the milk mixture. Bring to the boil, stirring all the time, until the sauce thickens. Combine with the cooked leeks and plenty of chopped fresh parsley, and season with salt and pepper. Divide into 10cm (4in) ramekins, lightly press on the topping and bake in the oven for 20 minutes until the top is crisp and golden. Mix the two ingredients of the topping together and season with salt and pepper.

In the summer these individual ramekins can be served with a side salad or in the winter with a jacket potato.

Parsnip and Cashew Bake

1 tablespoon olive oil	150ml (6fl oz) vegetable stock (use 1
1 medium onion, finely chopped	stock cube, make up from
170g (6oz) cashew nuts, roasted	bouillon powder or the fresh
115g (4oz) wholemeal	stock recipe on p.23)
breadcrumbs	the leaves from a sprig each of fresh
1 egg, beaten	rosemary and thyme
900g (2lb) parsnips, cooked	1 teaspoon yeast extract
and mashed	

Preheat oven: 160°C, 350°F; gas mark 4.

Line a 900g (2lb) loaf tin with baking parchment. Sauté the onion in the olive oil until soft, then combine all the ingredients and mix thoroughly. Place in the tin, smooth the top and cook uncovered for 30 minutes. Serve hot.

Kitchen Garden Crumble

1 tablespoon olive oil plus a little extra to oil dish
1 onion, finely chopped
1 clove of garlic, crushed
225g (8oz) leeks, sliced
2 courgettes, sliced

1 red pepper, de-seeded and chopped
450g (1lb) tomatoes, peeled and roughly chopped
A few leaves of fresh sage
Salt and pepper to taste

Topping
115g (4oz) rolled oats
50g (2oz) margarine or butter

50g (2oz) mature cheese, grated

Preheat oven: 160°C, 350°F; gas mark 4.

Sauté the onion and garlic in the oil until soft, add the rest of the vegetables and the sage leaves, season with salt and pepper to taste and cook gently for a couple of minutes. Place in an oiled ovenproof dish, sprinkle with the oats, diced margarine or butter and grated cheese. Bake uncovered for 30 minutes by which time the top should be nicely browned. Serve piping hot.

Spiced Vegetables and Rice

450g (1lb) brown rice, cooked in vegetable stock
2 onions, finely chopped
10ml (2 teaspoons) turmeric
2 cloves of garlic, crushed
50g (2oz) butter
1 large green pepper, chopped
170g (6oz) carrots, finely diced

115g (4oz) halved button mushrooms
pinch each of cinnamon, ginger and Chinese pure spice
50g (2oz) split toasted almonds
25g (1oz) sesame seeds, toasted
50g (2oz) sultanas
salt and pepper
plenty of chopped parsley

In a large saucepan, fry the finely chopped onion, turmeric and garlic in the butter. Add the pepper, carrots, mushrooms and spices and continue to cook over a low heat until the vegetables are just tender. Stir frequently with a wooden spoon. Cool the mixture before adding the almonds, sesame seeds and sultanas and season with salt and pepper. Very carefully fold this mixture into the cooked rice together with the chopped parsley, then turn out on to a large serving dish. It can be served either hot or cold.

Maureen Smith invented this recipe during a heatwave; it is light but spicy to tickle jaded palates.

Mushroom and Broad Bean Gougère

Choux pastry

115g (4oz) butter	4 eggs, lightly beaten
300ml (10fl oz) water	140g (5oz) cheese, grated
140g (5oz) plain flour	salt and pepper

Filling

75g (3oz) butter	225g (8oz) sliced mushrooms
50g (2oz) plain flour	tossed in butter
400ml (¾ pint) milk	salt and pepper
225g (8oz) fresh or frozen broad beans, cooked	

Preheat oven: 220°C, 425°F; gas mark 7.

Place the butter and water in a saucepan and heat gently until the butter has melted, then bring to the boil. Remove from the heat and add the flour all at once, beating well with a wooden spoon. Return the pan to a low heat and continue beating for around a minute until you have a smooth ball of paste that leaves the sides of the saucepan clean. Beat in the eggs a little at a time until you have a smooth glossy paste. Add 115g (4oz) grated cheese and season with salt and pepper.

Spoon dessertspoonfuls of the mixture around the edge of a large shallow ovenproof dish, sprinkle on the remainder of the cheese and bake for about 40 minutes, until the gougère is puffed up and golden brown.

For the filling make a parsley sauce: melt the butter in a saucepan, stir in the flour and cook for a minute or two before pouring in the milk. Stirring all the time, bring to the boil, then add a generous amount of parsley. Fold in the cooked vegetables and spoon into the centre of the gougère (if there is any over, offer it separately). Serve straight away.

Spinach, Fresh Herb and Cream Cheese Roulade

50g (2oz) butter or margarine	4 eggs, separated
50g (2oz) plain flour	225g (8oz) spinach, cooked, well drained and chopped
500ml (1 pint) milk	

Filling

225g (8oz) cream cheese	Fresh mixed herbs (suggestions, parsley, basil, tarragon or coriander) to taste
75ml (3oz) whipping cream	

Preheat oven: 180°C, 350°F; gas mark 4.

Line a Swiss roll tin 20cm × 15cm (8in × 6in) with baking parchment. Melt butter or margarine in a saucepan, add the flour and cook for a few minutes. Gradually beat in the milk, return to the boil stirring constantly. Take off the heat, cover with cling film to stop a skin forming and leave to cool. Beat the egg yolks and whisk the egg whites until stiff. When the sauce is nearly cool, place in a large bowl; beat in the egg yolks and the chopped spinach. Finally fold in the egg whites, slowly and carefully so as not to lose air.

Bake 20–30 minutes until the roulade is firm to the touch. Turn out on to a sheet of greaseproof paper and cool. Mix together the cream cheese, cream and herbs, season to taste and spread on the cooled roulade. Roll up lengthways. Serve in slices with a crisp mixed salad as a light meal.

Carrot, Courgette and Caraway Cake

125ml (5fl oz) vegetable oil
125g (5oz) caster sugar
3 eggs, beaten
125ml (5oz) self-raising flour sifted with 5ml (1 teaspoon) each of bicarbonate of soda, cinnamon and caraway seeds

75g (3oz) chopped mixed nuts
25g (1oz) desiccated coconut
115g (4oz) grated carrot
75g (3oz) grated courgette

Preheat oven: 180°C, 350°F; gas mark 4.

Line a 900g (2lb) loaf tin with baking parchment. In a large bowl, whisk together oil, sugar and eggs for about ten minutes. Gradually fold in the rest of the ingredients, alternating the nuts, vegetables with spoonfuls of the flour, bicarbonate and spices. Tip the mixture into the tin and bake for approximately 50 minutes. Turn out on to a wire rack and cool.

If you want to ice the cake, wait until it is cold and then use the topping under Drogo Carrot Cake on p.47.

Erddig

A 'pious, temperate, sensible country gentleman' – Simon Yorke I died in 1767 but his epitaph perfectly describes the Simons and Philips (eldest Yorke sons were invariably christened with one of these names), squires of Erddig for the next two centuries. They were also antiquarians, conservationists and the best of employers, leaving a unique record in writing, pictures and photographs of their servants and their way of life.

At Erddig, visitors enter the house, appropriately, by the back door after an extensive and fascinating tour of the buildings necessary to the running of a large estate. Some are still in use; the joiners' shop and the smithy hum with activity. The Yorkes did not believe in obsolescence: in the stables and wagon shed are aged bicycles, a 1907 Rover, 1920s Austins and nineteenth-century estate carts that were still in use in 1930. Beyond the stables is the female servants' preserve, comprising bakehouse, wet laundry, dry laundry (still fitted with huge racks and mangles) and, finally, the hub of this busy world, the New (in 1774) Kitchen. The kitchen is a wonderful room painted a peculiar shade of blue against flies, the great windows overlooking the garden, reflecting the Yorkes' unusual concern for the well-being of their staff. This interest in the staff continues in the basement passage, which is lined with nineteenth-century photographs, each with an appropriate verse penned by Philip II. Past the housekeeper's room, the agent's office and the still-room lies the servants' hall, again lined with portraits, this time eighteenth- and early nineteenth-century paintings with verses by Simon II. The carpenter, woodman, housemaid, and a black coach-boy are all celebrated here. Recent research has revealed that the coach-boy's name was John Hanby and his portrait dates from the first half of the eighteenth century.

And so at last, the green baize door is reached and above stairs.

Erddig is not a grand house, but the Yorkes loved it and filled it with treasures. Perhaps the grandest room is Thomas Hopper's Dining Room, lined with portraits of all the owners of Erddig since 1716 – except one. Here, and in the Saloon, Library, Entrance Hall and Drawing Room can be found fine furniture and china. Simon II, the missing owner, hangs in the delicate Chinese Room. Upstairs, the survival of the State Bed, despite a perilous eighteenth-century journey and neglect and rainwater in the twentieth century, is one of the wonders of Erddig. Now happily restored, its embroidery hangings glitter in a room lined with exquisite Chinese wallpaper. Upstairs, too, are little servants' rooms under the eaves of the house, a nursery full of toys, and a dark gallery adorned with eighteenth-century mother-of-pearl models created by Elizabeth Ratcliffe, an artistic lady's maid to Mrs Yorke.

Stroll in the formal garden, then climb the stairs to the restaurant in the old hay barn, often passing the delicious smell of freshly baked bread. Many interesting old recipes exist in the Erddig archives: the asparagus soup now served at Erddig is a really tasty adaptation, and others are reproduced here with more manageable quantities and instructions.

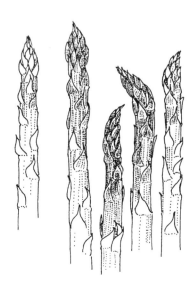

Asparagus Soup

1 bundle fresh asparagus (about 450g [1 lb])	50g (2oz) flour
125g (4oz) butter	400ml (¾ pint) extra strong vegetable stock (double strength)
1 small onion	salt and freshly ground black pepper
400ml (¾ pint) vegetable stock	250ml (½ pint) double cream

Remove the asparagus tips and reserve for garnishing. Cut off the tough ends, scrape the stems clean and cut these into 2·5cm (1in) pieces. Melt the butter, add the asparagus pieces and chopped onion and cook until barely tender, stirring regularly. Add the ordinary vegetable stock and simmer until the stalks are cooked and soft. Stir in the flour, add the double stock and continue stirring until the soup comes to the boil. Pour into a food processor and blend until smooth.

Steam or simmer very gently in water the asparagus tips until cooked but still crunchy.

Return the soup to the saucepan and just before serving reheat. Pour into individual bowls, swirl in some double cream to give a marble effect and scatter the asparagus tips on top.

Carrot Soup

450g (1 lb) carrots	2·5ml (½ teaspoon) crushed coriander
1 large onion	30ml (2 tablespoons) ground rice
50g (2oz) butter	juice of two oranges
1·5 litres (2½ pints) vegetable stock	salt and pepper

Slice the carrots and onions thinly and sweat with the butter in a large saucepan with the lid on until soft. Pour in the stock and crushed coriander, bring to the boil and simmer for 15 minutes. Add the ground rice and orange juice and continue to simmer for a further half an hour. Liquidise in a blender or food processor, return to the pan and season to taste.

Asparagus Soup

Take a hundred of asparagus, put the greatest part of them with two lettuces into three quarts of water. Boil them till they are tender enough to pulp through a colander; they should be boiled two or three hours after they are put through the colander. Add the remainder of the asparagus, put some cream and flour to make it a sufficient thickness, add pepper and salt to your taste. The asparagus you put in last are to swim in the soup.

*c.*1765

Carrot Soup

Take ½ a pound of fresh butter, put it in a stew pan with a good handful of pepper and salt, add to it a good quantity of carrots, turnips, celery, lettuce and onions. Set it on the fire as you do for gravy – take care it does not burn – have ready a tea kettle of boiling water, pour it in and let them boil gently 3 or 4 hours. Then strain it through a strainer. It should be the thickness of pea soup.

As recommended by Mrs Bringloe of Ongar   *c.*1765

Broccoli Open Pie

Serves eight–ten

300 g (10 oz) wholewheat pastry (use the pastry recipe from Chirk, Country Cheese Tart, p.58)
170 g (6 oz) cheese, grated

900 g (2 lb) broccoli florets, blanched and drained
10 eggs
400 ml (¾ pint) double cream

Preheat oven: 220°C, 425°F; gas mark 7.

Line a 20×30·5 cm (8×12 in) ovenproof flan dish with the rolled out pastry. Cover the base with half the grated cheese. Evenly place the broccoli florets on top. Whisk the eggs until lightly beaten, add the double cream and continue to whisk until it is incorporated. Pour over the broccoli and sprinkle on the rest of the grated cheese. Bake in a hot oven for 45 minutes.

This is more than a light snack; it makes a substantial supper dish served with a salad or as part of a buffet. Chopped spinach could be used as an alternative to the broccoli.

Old English Baked Rice Pudding

115g (4oz) pudding rice
rind of 1 lemon
500ml (1 pint) milk
50g (2oz) caster sugar
4 eggs
50g (2oz) unsalted butter

50g (2oz) raisins
50g (2oz) sultanas
25g (1oz) chopped peel or glacé
  cherries
grated nutmeg

Preheat oven: 150°C, 300°F; gas mark 2.

In a large pan, bring plenty of water to the boil. Wash the rice, put this into the water and boil for 17 minutes exactly. Rinse the rice in a sieve under running cold water.

In a double boiler, infuse the lemon rind with the milk and sugar. Beat the eggs in a separate basin. Whisk in the hot milk and return the mixture to the pan, stirring all the time until the sauce coats the back of a spoon.

Take the pan off the heat (off the water, that is), add the butter, fruits and cold rice. Butter an ovenproof dish and pour the mixture into this. Stand the dish in a second dish or meat tin containing hot water. Grate a little nutmeg over the top and bake for half an hour or until the pudding is set.

If you wish, this can be served with pouring cream.

This old-fashioned recipe was recommended by the great champion of English food, the late Michael Smith.

Cherry Conserve

900g (2lb) dark red cherries
juice and rind of 2 lemons
800g (1¾lb) sugar with pectin

30–45ml (2–3 tablespoons) cherry
  brandy or kirsch

Stone the cherries and place them with the rind and lemon juice in a large, heavy-based saucepan. Simmer very gently for about 15 minutes or until really soft, stirring from time to time to prevent them from sticking. Add the sugar and stir over a low heat until dissolved. Increase the heat and boil rapidly until setting point is reached (approximately another 5 minutes). Stir in the alcohol of your choice, then ladle into the prepared jars and cover when cold with waxed discs and cellophane secured with rubber bands. Makes 1·4–1·8kg (3–4lb).

This makes a delicious, slightly runny conserve.

> ### To Make a Rice Pudding
>
> Take half a pound of rice and steep it in new milk a whole night, and in the morning drain the milk away, then take a quart of the sweetest cream and put the rice into it and boil it a little. Then sit it to cool an hour or two and put in the yolks of half a dozen eggs, a little clove and mace, currants and sugar, mix them well together, put in great store of suet, boil them and serve them after a day old.
>
> *c.*1685
>
> ### To Preserve Cherries
>
> Take of the best and fairest cherries. Take some two pound and with a pair of shears clip off their stalks by the middle then wash them clean and beware you bruise them not, then take of fine barbery sugar and set it over the fire with a quart of water. Let it seethe till it be something thick then put in your cherries and stir them together with a silver spoon and so let them boil always stirring and skimming them. To know when they be enough you must take up some of the syrup with one cherry and let it cool and if it is enough it will scarce run out. When they are cold put them up.
>
> *c.*1685

Wholemeal Bread

250 ml (½ pint) tepid water
5 ml (1 teaspoon) sugar
10 ml (2 teaspoons) dried yeast
    (12 g [½oz] fresh yeast)

450 g (1 lb) 100% wholemeal flour
    or 350 g (12 oz) wholewheat flour
    and 115 g (4 oz) strong plain white
    flour
7·5 ml (1½ teaspoons) salt
12 g (½oz) vegetarian lard

Preheat oven: 200°C, 400°F; gas mark 6.

If using the dried yeast, place half the tepid water in a measuring jug and dissolve the sugar. Sprinkle the yeast over the top and leave in a warm place for 5–10 minutes until frothy (fresh yeast can be mixed in the water and used straight away). Put the flours and salt into a mixing bowl and rub in the fat. Add the frothed-up yeast and the balance of the water and mix with a wooden spoon to give a fairly soft dough (add more water if necessary). Turn out on to a clean work surface and knead for 10 minutes until the dough is smooth and supple. Place in a well-greased 450 g (1 lb) loaf tin, pushing the dough well down into the corners and sides of the tin to encourage it to form a dome-shaped loaf. Put the tin in a warm place covered with a damp tea towel or placed in a lightly greased polythene bag, tied loosely, and leave to rise for 30–40 minutes or until the loaf has doubled in size and within 6 mm (¼ in) of the top of the bread tin.

If you wish, the surface of the loaf can be sprinkled with poppy seeds, sesame seeds, rolled oats or crack wheat. Brush the dough lightly with water or beaten egg to make the seeds stick.

Bake in the oven for about 40 minutes. Turn out the bread and, if cooked, the loaf will sound hollow when tapped underneath. Leave to cool on a wire tray.

Barley Water

50 g (2 oz) pearl barley	2 lemons
1·25 litres (2 pints) water	sugar to taste

Wash the barley and put it to boil with the water and the thinly peeled rinds of the lemons. Boil very gently for 2 hours, then strain. Add sugar to taste, stir to dissolve it and leave to cool. Just before serving, add the juice from the 2 lemons.

Barley water was thought to be medicinal but there is no proof of this. However, as the old recipe suggests, it is a pleasantly cooling drink.

A Dainty Cooling Drink for a Hot Fever

Take French barley one ounce, boil it first in a quart of fair water a good while, then shift it and boil it in another quart of water a good while. Shift it again and boil it in a bottle of fair spring water to a quart, then take two ounces of sweet almonds, lay them to soak all night then stamp and strain them in the last barley water. Put to it 4 spoonsful of damask rose water, the juice of one lemon and with sugar sweeten it to your taste. Drink of this often when you are dry or hot.

c.1685

Kedleston Hall

Kedleston Hall is one of the grandest houses in England. It was planned, built and furnished in the 1760s, the magnificent result of a collaboration between two young men, Nathaniel Curzon, 1st Lord Scarsdale and the Scottish architect Robert Adam. Tracing the plans of these two men takes one's breath away with the effrontery of the idea and scale of the task they took on, but probably older and more cautious men would not have achieved the splendid marriage between great house and great landscape that particularly distinguishes Kedleston.

First, the old village was swept away and the highway moved. The canals and ponds were re-dug as lakes and cascades, the old formal gardens landscaped into the park. Visitors approach down a long drive; as you cross the two lakes over an elegant three-arched bridge, the north front of the house appears before you, described as 'the grandest Palladian facade in Britain with few rivals anywhere in the world'. A dramatic portico dominates the central block, with great wings to left and right. It is an awe-inspiring sight. From the day he finished the house, Lord Scarsdale opened the main rooms at Kedleston for visitors to admire. Today, visitors see the identical rooms, furnished and decorated to Adam's original designs. The Marble Hall and Saloon are the great receiving rooms, flanked on the one side by the arts – Music Room, Drawing Room and Library – and on the other by hospitality, the Dining Room and the principal apartment for important guests. The decoration is elaborate but not heavy in the pastel colours originally specified; Scarsdale's collection of pictures hang in the same spaces they were allotted in the original arrangement. Adam's furnishings can still arouse awe and admiration with his almost sensual use of gilt and rich silks. Huge pier glasses increase the architectural vistas.

Golden plumes crown the mirrors, while the state bed is a riot of palm trees and fronds. Most wonderful of all are the huge, damask-covered drawing-room sofas made for Adam by the cabinetmaker John Linnell, and supported by voluptuous tritons and sea-nymphs. Here, too, is evidence of young Adam's confidence, coupled with his Scot's concern for extravagance: the gold decorations on the skirting and dado stop behind the sofas and the walls are not painted behind the pictures. It would be no surprise to Adam to find everything in its place two centuries later.

Curzons have lived at Kedleston since the twelfth century and their portraits line the walls of the Family Corridor, together with a family tree seen in the balancing Kitchen Corridor. Descending the Grand Staircase leads to an Eastern Museum housing a collection of Indian furniture and objects built up by Lord Curzon, who was Viceroy of India from 1899 to 1905.

Through the shop and along the Exhibition Corridor lies the Great Kitchen, '48 feet by 24 feet and very lofty' noted Sir Christopher Sykes in 1794. Here, below a gallery supported on fine Doric columns, lunches and teas are served using the original two huge scrubbed kitchen tables. Robert Adam would have approved of the motto 'Waste Not, Want Not' over the giant range and spit.

Country Vegetable Soup

25g (1oz) butter	450g (1lb) potatoes
2 red peppers, chopped	milk (optional)
115g (4oz) carrots, sliced	salt and pepper
115g (4oz) swede, chopped	freshly chopped parsley
115g (4oz) sweetcorn	a few spring onion tops, chopped

The weights for vegetables are just a guideline – you need to end up with 700g (1½lb) vegetables (excluding potatoes).

In a saucepan melt the butter and sweat all the vegetables, except the potatoes, until cooked. Peel the potatoes and barely cover them with water and boil until soft. Drain, reserving the cooking liquid, and mash until creamy. Return to the saucepan with the cooking liquid and vegetables and stir together. Thin if necessary with milk. Season with salt and pepper, reheat and serve piping hot, sprinkled with parsley and a few chopped onion tops.

Sweet 'n Sour Mushrooms

To fill four ramekins

350g (12oz) button mushrooms	5ml (1 teaspoon) wholegrain mustard
25g (1oz) butter	200ml (⅓ pint) double cream
10ml (1 dessertspoon) creamed horseradish	salt and pepper
5ml (1 teaspoon) redcurrant jelly	

Chop any large mushrooms in half and sauté gently in the butter for two or three minutes. Cool slightly. Combine all the other ingredients in a bowl – use a small whisk to mix in the redcurrant jelly. Season with salt and pepper. Pack the mushrooms into the ramekins and pour over the sauce.

Serve as an *hors d'oeuvre* with chunky bread to soak up the juice. It can be served warm on a cold day.

Courgette Tart

Pastry
115g (4oz) plain white flour
pinch salt
25g (1oz) butter or margarine

25g (1oz) vegetarian lard
cold water

Filling
50g (2oz) butter
1 medium onion, chopped
225g (8oz) courgettes, sliced
2·5ml (½ teaspoon) savory (or
   other herb of your choice)

2 eggs, lightly beaten
150ml (¼ pint) creamy milk
30ml (2 tablespoons) Parmesan
   cheese, grated

Preheat oven: 180°C, 350°F; gas mark 4.

Sift the flour and salt into a mixing bowl. Cut the fat into small cubes and add to the flour. Using your fingertips, lightly rub the fat into the flour until the mixture looks uniformly crumbly. Sprinkle on 30ml (2 tablespoons) cold water and draw together with a knife to bring the pastry together, adding a little more water if necessary. Then with your hands, form a smooth ball dough that leaves the sides of the bowl clean. Roll out the pastry and line a greased 18cm (7in) flan tin. Prick with a fork and bake for 15 minutes on a preheated baking sheet in the centre of the oven.

For the filling, melt the butter in a saucepan and sweat the onion for a few minutes, add the courgettes and savory and continue to cook until the courgettes are just tender.

Place the onion and courgettes in the pastry case. Mix together the eggs, milk, 1 tablespoon of the Parmesan cheese and salt and pepper and pour over the top. Sprinkle over the remaining Parmesan cheese and bake for 30 minutes.

Fresh Orange Dressing

juice 1½ oranges
5ml (1 teaspoon) orange rind
15ml (1 tablespoon) sunflower oil

1 clove of garlic, crushed
salt and pepper

A very simple recipe – just mix together all the ingredients and use with any salad. It would go well with Buckland Abbey Carrot, Raisin and Sesame Seed Salad on p.30. Makes sufficient to dress a bowl of salad for four.

Potted Mushrooms

Makes 4 ramekins

350g (12oz) button mushrooms
50g (2oz) butter
1 level teaspoon mace

Salt and pepper to taste
25-50g (1-2oz) clarified butter

Slice mushrooms thinly. Melt butter in saucepan and stew the mushrooms gently until soft. Drain and squeeze out as much liquid as possible, cool. When the mushrooms are cold, press down into small pots or ramekins, leaving 2·5cms, (¹/₂ inch) at the top. Clarify the extra butter as follows: heat the butter in a small pan until it is foaming. Allow it to stand – pour off the butter over each ramekin leaving behind the sediment in the small pan. This will seal the pots which will keep for a few days in the fridge. Serve with toast or French bread, and a salad.

Cheese and Onion Bread and Butter Pudding

3 medium slices of white bread
3 medium slices of wholemeal bread
50g (2oz) softened butter
1 large onion, peeled and thinly sliced
225g (8oz) curd cheese
2 eggs

625ml (1¼ pints) full cream milk
¼ teaspoon English mustard
  powder
Salt and pepper to taste
25g (1oz) chopped walnuts

To finish: Finely chopped spring onions or chives

Preheat oven: 160°C, 325°F; gas mark 3.

Spread the slices of bread with the butter. Make 3 sandwiches, using the chopped onion and cheese as a filling. Use one slice of wholemeal and one sliced of white for each sandwich. Press firmly together and cut each sandwich into 4 triangles. Place in a shallow ovenproof dish with the points facing upwards.

Beat together the eggs, milk, mustard powder and seasoning. Pour over the sandwiches and leave to stand for 30 minutes.
Scatter the walnuts over the pudding and bake for approximately 45 minutes, or until set with a crisp golden topping. Sprinkle with spring onions or chives and serve.

This is a local Derbyshire recipe. It is an excellent way to use up yesterday's bread. It also tastes good made with leeks.

Onion and Cheese Swirl Loaf

Brown bread dough (use the
Wholemeal Bread recipe from
Erddig on p.79). Place in a greased
polythene bag to rise instead of in
a loaf tin.

25g (1 oz) butter
2 small onions, chopped
115g (4 oz) Red Leicester cheese,
grated fresh herbs of your choice
salt and pepper
paprika

Preheat oven: 230°C, 450°F; gas mark 8.

Once the dough has finished 'proving', take out of the polythene bag and roll out on a clean working surface into a rectangle approximately 20×35·5cm (8×14in).

Melt the butter and sweat the chopped onions until transparent. Spread them along the length of the dough piece together with the grated cheese and herbs. Season well with salt and pepper and roll up firmly like a Swiss roll and place on to a greased baking tray. Place the tray inside the polythene bag and once again leave to rise for 30 minutes. Take out of the bag, dust the top with paprika, and bake in a hot oven for 50–60 minutes.

This makes an ideal accompaniment to soup or a salad.

Sweet Potato Bake

500g (1 lb 2 oz) sweet potatoes
25g (1 oz) cinnamon
115g (4 oz) grated Sage Derby
Cheese

115g (4 oz) grated Cheddar cheese
2 eggs
60ml (2 fl oz) milk
1 dessertspoon caster sugar

Preheat oven: 190°C, 375,°F; gas mark 5.

Peel and dice the sweet potatoes into large chunks, put in a pan with enough water to cover. Bring to the boil and simmer until tender (be careful not to overcook them). Drain and place in a well-buttered flan dish. Sprinkle with the cinnamon and then with the two grated cheeses. Mix the eggs with the milk and pour over the potatoes and cheese. Sprinkle the top with the sugar. Bake for approximately 20 to 30 minutes until the top is golden brown.

This is a nineteenth-century recipe. If you can't find Sage Derby, use another mild crumbly cheese. Anne Parkin, who gave me this recipe, likes to use a Sage Derby that is made locally, in which the sage is particularly piquant. If you have to use another cheese you could add a leaf or two of fresh sage finely chopped at the same time as the cinnamon.

Kingston Lacy

The lives of the Bankes family have been woven into the fabric of Kingston Lacy since Sir John Bankes, Charles I's Chief Justice, bought the land on which the present house is built, together with Corfe Castle. Fortunes fluctuate: Sir John's wife, brave Dame Mary, whose statue dominates the first flight of the marble staircase at Kingston Lacy, withstood two Civil War sieges at Corfe before the castle was sacked and ruined; her son, Sir Ralph, back in favour, built a new family seat at Kingston Lacy in mellow red brick, the bones of today's house. He also laid the foundation of Kingston Lacy's glory, the magnificent collection of paintings. Kingston Lacy is no soulless gallery, however; the Bankes family loved their house and altered and improved it whilst adding to the Lelys and Van Dycks of Sir Ralph's original collection.

No one did more for Kingston Lacy than William John Bankes, 'the father of all mischiefs' according to his bosom friend, Lord Byron. He and architect Sir Charles Barry transformed Kingston Lacy into the handsome house we see today. They faced it with Chilmark stone, fashioned a new classical entrance hall, a sumptuous marble staircase and loggia as a setting for William's collection of bronzes and marbles, and arranged the state rooms in today's pattern. An enthusiastic traveller and explorer, William sent home a rich variety of treasures, including Sebastian del Piombo's masterpiece *The Judgement of Solomon* which dominates the Dining Room.

The great Saloon has pictures banked three deep on every wall, notably two aristocratic Italian beauties by Rubens and a noble Titian. He erected the obelisk of Philae in the grounds, constructed a jewel of a room hung in leather to display his Spanish collection, and bought carvings and furniture.

Banished abroad in disgrace for a sexual indiscretion, he nevertheless continued to commission fittings in wood and marble, shipping them home and writing long letters to his sister on where to put them, until his death in 1855.

Another formidable lady left her mark on the Drawing Room: Henrietta Bankes reigned, first as wife, then during a long widowhood from 1904. The room is just as she decorated it with rose damask walls, French furniture and a clutter of workboxes, miniatures, plants and ornaments. It was her son, Ralph, who bequeathed the house and all its contents to the Trust, one of the greatest legacies it has ever received.

Beyond the kitchen courtyard are the red-brick stables where visitors can now have the unusual experience of eating in a private loose-box complete with manger and hay basket, or on a fine day in the stable yard. Recipes include good soups, a particularly delicious lasagne and a chocolate muesli bar too good to miss.

Garlic, then have the power to save from death
Bear with it though it maketh unsavoury breath
And scorn not garlic like some that think
It only maketh men wink and drink and stink.

The Englishman's Doctor, Sir John Harington (1609)

Tomato and Cheese Soup

2 medium onions, finely chopped	10 ml (1 dessertspoon) red wine vinegar
50 g (2 oz) butter	500 ml (1 pint) milk
25 g (1 oz) flour	salt and pepper
170 g (6 oz) tomato purée	75 g (3 oz) Cheddar cheese, grated
500 ml (1 pint) vegetable stock	parsley, chopped

In a large saucepan, sauté the finely chopped onions in butter until soft. Stir in the flour and cook for a minute or two before adding the tomato purée, vegetable stock and red wine vinegar. Bring to the boil, stirring all the time and simmer for 5–10 minutes. Take off the heat and blend in a food processor (alternatively, it tastes just as good left as it is). Return to the pan, pour in the milk and season with salt and pepper. Reheat the soup, but don't let it boil, and stir in half the grated Cheddar cheese. Ladle into individual bowls and top with the remainder of the grated cheese and finely chopped parsley mixed together.

Economical and fast, yet with a subtle tangy flavour – a useful recipe as it consists of only staples from the store cupboard.

Curried Brown Rice Salad

170 g (6 oz) brown rice	15 ml (1 tablespoon) curry powder combined with 90 ml (6 tablespooons) French dressing
50 g (2 oz) coarsely chopped walnuts	
50 g (2 oz) raisins	15 ml (1 tablespoon) parsley, freshly chopped
2 eating apples, chopped	

Cook the rice as described on the packet, drain and allow to cool slightly. In a salad bowl combine the walnuts, raisins, chopped apple and curry dressing. When the rice is lukewarm, tip it into the bowl and gently mix with the other ingredients with a wooden spoon. Lastly sprinkle on the chopped parsley for added colour. A nutty, spicy salad.

Mushroom and Tarragon Salad

450g (1 lb) mushrooms
10 ml (1 dessertspoon) dried tarragon
(or fresh if you have it)

120 ml (8 tablespoons) vinaigrette
dressing
salt and pepper

Wipe the mushrooms if necessary and slice. Gently mix in the tarragon, vinaigrette dressing and salt and pepper.

Good too, made with fresh mint if tarragon isn't available.

Carrot and Coconut Salad

450g (1 lb) carrots
45 ml (3 tablespoons) desiccated
coconut
2·5 ml (½ teaspoon) ground ginger

50g (2 oz) sultanas
60 ml (4 tablespoons) vinaigrette
dressing
salt and freshly ground black pepper

Peel and coarsely grate the carrots. Mix all the other ingredients together and season with salt and pepper.

Economical and exotic!

The cookery and household books belonging to Henrietta Bankes are preserved at Kingston Lacy. Henrietta was the wife of Walter Ralph Bankes, and came to Kingston Lacy after her marriage in 1897. Here is her recipe for 'anyone overworked or below par':

50g (2oz) salsaperella
50g (2oz) peruvian bark
12g (½oz) gentian root
225g (½lb) sugar candy

250ml (½ pint) black beer
400ml (¾ pint) old rum
1·25 litres (2 pints) cold water
500ml (1 pint) hot water

Place 1·25 litre (2 pints) cold water with the herbs on the oven all night. Strain off the liquid next morning, then rinse with 500ml (1 pint) boiling water, and after again straining, boil both the pints and the quarts of water with the sugar candy until the candy is dissolved. When cold, add the black beer and rum. 1 wineglass in a morning and evening if required.

Vegetarian Lasagne

Vegetable Sauce

50 g (2 oz) butter
1 onion, finely chopped
1 clove of garlic, crushed
1 red or green pepper, diced
350 g (12 oz) mixed vegetables, chopped (courgettes, carrots, French beans, peas, broad beans)

115 g (4 oz) tinned or frozen sweetcorn
1 small tin tomatoes
30 ml (2 tablespoons) tomato purée
2·5 ml (1 teaspoon) dried oregano
115 g (4 oz) tinned, drained kidney beans
salt and pepper

Béchamel Sauce

37 g (1½ oz) butter
37 g (1½ oz) flour
400 ml (¾ pint) milk

grated nutmeg
salt and pepper

Topping

115 g (4 oz) Parmesan and Cheddar cheese, grated and mixed to dust on the lasagne layers

Lasagne

350 g (12 oz) oven-ready or pre-cooked lasagne

Preheat oven: 190°C, 375°F; gas mark 5.

Melt the butter in a large saucepan and fry the onion for 10 minutes until soft but not browned. Add the garlic, diced pepper and the chopped vegetables and continue to fry for a few minutes, stirring now and then before mixing in the sweetcorn, tinned tomatoes, tomato purée and the oregano. Place a lid on the pan and simmer for 20 minutes or until the vegetables are tender. Take off the heat, stir in the drained kidney beans and season with salt and pepper.

To make the sauce, melt the butter in a saucepan, stir in the flour and cook for a minute or two before pouring in the milk. Stirring all the time, bring to the boil, then add the nutmeg, salt and pepper.

Have the pasta and sauce all ready. Put a layer of the vegetable sauce on the bottom of an ovenproof dish. Cover with a thin layer of béchamel sauce, dust with cheese and place a layer of lasagne sheets on top. Continue like this until all the ingredients are used up, ending with the béchamel sauce, sprinkled with cheese.

Bake in the oven for 30–40 minutes until the top is golden.

Chocolate Muesli Bar

75g (3oz) butter
15ml (1 tablespoon) golden syrup
225g (8oz) muesli
50g (2oz) dates, chopped

50g (2oz) dried apricots, chopped
50g (2oz) walnuts and almonds, chopped
115g (4oz) plain chocolate

Melt the butter and golden syrup in a saucepan. Remove from the heat and add all the ingredients except the chocolate. Press into a rectangular or square tin and allow to set. Very gently melt the chocolate and spread over the biscuit mixture. Allow to set once again, then cut into fingers.

Dorset Apple Cake

225g (8oz) eating apples
115g (4oz) butter
115g (4oz) demerara sugar
225g (8oz) self-raising flour

5ml (1 teaspoon) ground cinnamon
2 eggs, lightly beaten
icing sugar

Preheat oven: 180°C, 350°F; gas mark 4.

Grease and line a 20cm (8in) cake tin. Peel, core and roughly chop the apples. In a mixing bowl, cream together the butter and sugar until light and fluffy. Sieve the flour and cinnamon and add alternately with the eggs into the sugar and butter; adding these ingredients alternately stops the eggs curdling. Stir in the chopped apple and spoon into the prepared tin.

Bake in the oven for 50 minutes. Cool slightly before turning out on to a wire rack to cool. When cold, dust the top with icing sugar. Good served warm as a pudding with some clotted cream.

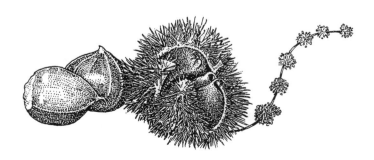

Montacute House

Montacute is a golden Elizabethan house, a wonderful amalgam of Gothic and Renaissance. Sir Edward Phelips, a successful lawyer, built the house in the last years of the sixteenth century with the help of a Somerset mason, William Arnold. Arnold was able to introduce the latest Renaissance detail – shell-headed niches, obelisks and a symmetrical plan – yet the house remains firmly embedded in the Gothic, with reminders of chivalric pageantry, romantic evocations beloved by the Elizabethans.

Beyond the outbuildings and kitchen gardens lies the village of Montacute, with the sharp hill, *mons acutus*, that gives the village and the house their name. Beyond the formal gardens and tree-lined avenues is the green countryside of Somerset, sheep and somnolent cows grazing peacefully in a quintessentially English landscape.

The Phelips family lived there for three centuries. As their fortunes waxed and waned, so did Montacute's, sometimes richly furnished and sometimes neglected. Wills of byzantine complexity and family squabbles decimated the Phelips' inheritance, so that by the twentieth century the estate was insolvent. After years of letting, the house was in such poor repair that in 1931 it was valued for £5,882 'for scrap' and in grave danger of demolition. Montacute was rescued and given to the Trust, but the problem of furnishing the house remained. Generous individuals and organisations have lent or given furniture, pictures and furnishings so that the rooms are now furnished in appropriately spare fashion. Phelips portraits from every century watch today's visitors admiring the impressive stone screen in the hall, the intriguing plasterwork and the massive Ham stone fireplaces. Lord Curzon, a famous tenant, is remembered by a bedroom containing a huge bath in a Jacobean-style cupboard, the nearest to modern convenience to be found in this very traditional house.

Climb the stairs to the second floor to find the largest Long Gallery to survive in England: 172 feet long with oriel windows at each end giving wonderful views of garden and countryside. The National Portrait Gallery has hung here a fascinating collection of Tudor and Jacobean portraits. Beautiful and ugly, noble and not so noble, happy and sad, the faces bring to life those who influenced this turbulent period of English history.

In bad weather, the Elizabethans used the Long Gallery for gentle exercise. When fine, they strolled in the walled gardens as we do today, admiring the grand façades of the great house, the beautifully clipped hedges and well-kept beds. Behind a huge yew hedge planted to allow servants to reach the kitchen gardens (now the car parks) unobserved, you will find the old laundry and bakehouse, now the restaurant. Old mullioned windows, low ceilings and pink lacy tablecloths provide a homely background to carefully cooked, imaginative recipes. Local ingredients feature largely. In Golden Cider Soup, local cider is an essential ingredient which produces one of the best soups I have ever tasted.

While the Phelips family were enjoying a good diet in their great house at Montacute, with plenty of fresh fruit and vegetables produced by the extensive kitchen garden, their tenants in the adjacent village were faring less well. An extract from *The Skeleton at the Plough, 1827–46*, an autobiographical account by George Mitchell, gives some idea of their daily diet:

Our food consisted principally of a little barley-cake, potatoes, salt, tea kettle broth and barley 'flippet'. Tea kettle broth consisted of a few pieces of bread soaked in hot water with a little salt, sometimes with a leek chopped up in it. Never had I ever a sufficient quantity of bread being used for the spoon to stand upright in. Barley flippet was made by sprinkling barley-meal into a pot of boiling water which when sufficiently thickened was served up with salt and a little treacle.

Sometimes, I would pull a turnip from the field and gnaw it to prevent hunger ... If I could find peas, beans or carrots, I would eat as many as I could get and many a time have I hunted and foraged about for snails in the hedges and roasted them for my lunch and tea.

Golden Cider Soup

50 g (2 oz) butter
225 g (8 oz) carrots, diced
225 g (8 oz) potatoes, diced
2 cloves of garlic, crushed
400 g (14 oz) tin chopped tomatoes

400 ml (¾ pint) medium or sweet cider
400 ml (¾ pint) vegetable stock
salt and freshly ground pepper

Melt the butter in a large saucepan and sweat the diced carrots and potatoes for 5 minutes. Add the crushed garlic, tin of tomatoes, cider and vegetable stock and bring to the boil. Cover and simmer until the vegetables are tender. Season with salt and pepper. Pour into a food processor and blend until very smooth. Return to the pan and reheat before serving.

The cider gives this simple recipe a wonderful, luxurious flavour.

Salad Soup

1 onion, finely chopped	4 radishes, chopped
50g (2oz) butter	4 tomatoes, quartered
1 lettuce, shredded	2 punnets of mustard and cress
1 green pepper, diced	vegetable stock
½ cucumber, peeled and diced	salt and pepper

In a large saucepan sauté the chopped onion in the butter until soft. Add the shredded lettuce, diced green pepper, peeled and diced cucumber, chopped radishes, quartered tomatoes and most of the mustard and cress. Add sufficient vegetable stock to cover. Simmer until everything is soft, then blend in a food processor. Return to the saucepan to reheat before serving. Sprinkle the remainder of the mustard and cress as a garnish to each bowl.

An odd, distinctive flavour – a good soup if the weather turns suddenly cold in high summer.

Ratatouille

1 onion, coarsely chopped	60ml (4 tablespoons) olive oil
2 cloves of garlic, crushed	400g (14oz) tin tomatoes
1 small aubergine, diced into chunks	5ml (1 teaspoon) mixed herbs
2 courgettes, sliced	salt and freshly ground black pepper
115g (4oz) mushrooms, sliced	

In a large saucepan sauté the prepared vegetables in olive oil until they are beginning to soften. Add the tin of tomatoes and herbs, bring to the boil and then put a lid on the saucepan. Turn down the heat and leave to cook gently for 40 minutes. Season with salt and pepper before serving.

Use this recipe as a vegetable accompaniment or to stuff the pancakes from Berrington Hall on p.19.

Ratatouille Soup

Cool the above ratatouille mixture and blend in a food processor. Return to the saucepan and stir in 675ml (1¼ pints) vegetable stock. Reheat and serve piping hot, garnished with parsley. A truly Mediterranean flavour.

Rice and Cheese Terrine

225g (8oz) rice
50g (2oz) butter
1 onion, chopped
2 cloves of garlic, crushed
115g (4oz) mixed vegetables, diced
  (you can use frozen if in a hurry)

115–170g (4–6oz) cheese, grated
2 tomatoes, chopped
2 eggs, lightly beaten
salt and pepper
170g (6oz) red peppers, chopped

Preheat oven: 180°C, 350°F; gas mark 4.

Cook the rice, preferably in some vegetable stock, until tender. Melt the butter in a saucepan and sweat the onion and garlic until transparent. Cook the vegetables of your choice. In a mixing bowl combine all the ingredients, except the red peppers, and season well.

Line a 900g (2lb) loaf tin with non-stick paper. Layer half the rice mixture into the tin, spread over the chopped red peppers and add a final layer of the balance of the mixture. Cover with foil and bake in the oven for 1 hour. Cool slightly before turning out carefully and removing the lining paper.

Serve hot or cold.

Mushrooms and Red Wine Sauce

50g (2oz) butter
450g (1lb) button mushrooms –
  halves or quarters according
  to size

3 tomatoes
150ml (¼ pint) extra rich vegetable
  stock
150ml (¼ pint) red wine
salt and freshly ground black pepper

Melt the butter in a saucepan and cook the mushrooms for a minute or two, stirring frequently. Skin, de-seed and chop the tomatoes and add to the mushrooms with the balance of the ingredients. Simmer together for around 5 minutes, then take out approximately half the sauce and blend it in a food processor. Return the sauce to the pan and simmer with the mushroom mixture for another 10 minutes. Makes about 250ml (½ pint).

This is a rich sauce, perfect to accompany the Lentil and Wine Pâté from Cliveden, p.67 or, as an alternative to Spicy Tomato Topping, the Minty Nut Loaf from Castle Drogo, p.44.

Somerset Quiche

Pastry

75g (3oz) Cheddar cheese, grated	75g (3oz) butter or margarine
170g (6oz) plain flour	1 egg yolk
pinch of mustard	cold water
salt and pepper	

Filling

1 large onion, chopped	3 eggs
50g (2oz) butter	50g (2oz) clotted cream (or extra
115g (4oz) fresh white breadcrumbs	double cream if clotted
250ml (½ pint) milk	unobtainable)
2 bay leaves	salt and pepper

Preheat oven: 200°C, 400°F; gas mark 6.

Grate the Cheddar cheese. In a large mixing bowl place the flour, mustard and seasoning. Cut the fat into small cubes and rub into the flour, using your fingertips until the mixture resembles fine breadcrumbs. Tip in the grated cheese and combine well. Add the egg yolk and 15ml (one tablespoon) of cold water and draw together with a knife and then your fingers to form a dough (if necessary add a little more water). Knead slightly, then, ideally, chill in a polythene bag in the fridge for around 30 minutes.

Put a baking sheet into the centre of the oven to heat up. Roll out the pastry and line a greased 23cm (9in) tin. Prick the base all over, place on the baking sheet and bake for 15 minutes or until the pastry is firm.

Turn the oven down to 180°C, 350°F, gas mark 4. Sweat the chopped onion in the butter and place in the pastry case with the breadcrumbs. In a small saucepan infuse the milk with the bay leaves. Remove from the heat and pour over the breadcrumbs. Whisk together the eggs, clotted cream and seasoning and pour into the flan case. Place on the baking sheet and bake for 35–40 minutes or until the filling is set and lightly browned.

Fresh bay leaves are essential for the flavour.

Stilton and Walnut Quiche

300g (10oz) wholewheat pastry	115g (4oz) chopped walnuts
(use the recipe from Chirk,	3 eggs
Country Cheese Tart p.58)	250ml (½ pint) milk
170g (6oz) crumbled Stilton cheese	salt and pepper

Preheat oven: 180°C, 350°F; gas mark 4.
(Place a baking sheet in the centre.)

Prepare the pastry case as previously described.

Sprinkle the crumbled Stilton and chopped walnuts on the base of the case. Whisk together the eggs and milk and season well. Pour carefully into the flan and place in the centre of oven on the baking sheet. Bake for 40–45 minutes. Leave to cool for around 10–15 minutes to allow the filling to 'firm up' before serving.

Jo's Pickle

450g (1 lb) onions, peeled	450g (1 lb) soft brown sugar
675g (1½lb) cooking apples, peeled and cored	4ml (1 level teaspoon) salt
	pinch of cayenne
450g (1 lb) stoned dates	scant 500ml (1 pint) spiced or
450g (1 lb) sultanas	pickling vinegar

Coarsely chop the onions, apples and dates in a food processor (make sure you leave some texture) and place in a large mixing bowl. Add in the sultanas, sugar, salt and cayenne and pour on the vinegar. Mix well. Cover with a cloth overnight (add extra vinegar if necessary), pack into jars and cover with a waxed disc and cellophane. This will keep for around 6 months.

At Montacute it is served with Somerset Cheddar as a Ploughman's Lunch, but it also makes a good present for pickle lovers.

Rhubarb and Orange Tart

Pastry

115g (4oz) plain flour sifted with 2·5ml (½ teaspoon) cinammon and a pinch of salt	25g (1oz) caster sugar
	1 egg yolk
	15ml (1 tablespoon) cold water
75g (3oz) butter	

Filling

675g (1½lb) rhubarb	juice and rind of 1 orange
75g (3oz) dark brown sugar	

Topping

2 egg whites, beaten	115g (4oz) caster sugar

Preheat oven: 200°C, 400°F; gas mark 6.

Use the pastry instructions as for Lemon Tart from Chirk (p.59) and bake blind in a 20 cm (8 in) flan tin for 15–20 minutes.

To make the filling, cut the rhubarb into manageable lengths and place in a saucepan with the sugar and juice and rind of an orange. Heat gently and cook until barely tender (test for sweetness – you may need to add a little more sugar). Place in the pre-baked pastry case and set aside.

For the topping, beat together two egg whites until stiff and fold in 115 g (4 oz) caster sugar. Pile this on the pudding and bake for 15–20 minutes until pale brown and set. Serve hot or cold.

Somerset Cider Cake

225 g (8 oz) sultanas	2 eggs
150 ml (¼ pint) sweet or medium dry cider	225 g (8 oz) plain flour
115 g (4 oz) butter	5 ml (1 teaspoon) bicarbonate of soda
115 g (4 oz) soft light brown sugar	

Topping

75 g (3 oz) butter	5 ml (1 teaspoon) lemon juice
170 g (6 oz) icing sugar	15 ml (1 tablespoon) runny honey

Preheat oven: 180°C, 350°F; gas mark 4.

Grease and line a 20 cm (8 in) cake tin.

Soak the sultanas overnight in the cider. Cream together the butter and sugar until light and fluffy. Gradually beat in the eggs one at a time. Fold in half the flour and the bicarbonate of soda, then the sultanas and cider and lastly the balance of the flour.

Bake in the centre of the oven for approximately 1 hour or until a skewer comes out clean. Cool slightly before turning out on to a wire rack and remove the lining paper.

For the topping, whisk the butter until light. Add the balance of the ingredients and continue whisking until well combined. When the cake is completely cold, spoon on the topping and fork over until it looks like a candlewick bath mat!

Moseley Old Hall

Moseley Old Hall in Staffordshire is cared for by the National Trust because it has a special association with a particular person and period in English history.

From the outside, Moseley appears a small, nineteenth-century red-brick house; no clue here to its significance, though an expert on garden design might pause over the elaborate seventeenth-century knot garden.

But step through the heavily studded back door and you are in a timber-framed house of the middle years of the seventeenth century; more specifically the morning of 8 September 1651, when this modest house and its worthy but not aristocratic family, the Whitgreaves, were swept up in the bloody civil war then raging between Royalists and Parliamentarians. Charles I had been executed two years earlier, but his eldest son, Charles II, had met in battle Cromwell's forces at Worcester on 3 September and had been heavily defeated. On the run with £1,000 (a huge figure in those days) on his head, Charles finally reached Moseley. Thomas Whitgreave, 'The Preserver', and his mother, Dame Alice, were Catholics and Royalist sympathisers; they sheltered the desperate man for two days until his escape to Bristol and later to France, disguised as serving man to Jane Lane, a near neighbour. You can see the heartfelt letter of thanks he wrote Jane in the hall at Moseley.

Thomas wrote a detailed account of those two days, and, retracing Charles's steps through the house, the events still seem vivid. The house is furnished just as it would have been in 1651. In the bedroom is the heavy oak four-poster bed in which the exhausted man slept; through a door you can see the small hiding place into which tall Charles – he was over 6 foot – crammed his body when soldiers came to search the grounds and to interrogate Thomas. From the small windows above the porch he watched with Thomas and the local priest, Father John Huddlestone, the bedraggled remnants of his army making their slow way north back to Scotland. Under the eaves is the little oratory, a tranquil evocative room. Perhaps Charles experienced some spiritual solace here, for he called it 'a very decent place' and years later, when he was dying, summoned Father Huddlestone who received him into the Catholic faith and administered the last rites.

Portraits and mementoes bring alive those momentous events, and local schools today spend whole days at Moseley making seventeenth-century recipes and rushlights, and experiencing for themselves that earlier world. Outside, a seventeenth-century garden has been recreated, old herbaceous plants, shrubs and roses filling the beds; there is a formal knot garden and old varieties of fruit – quinces, mulberries and medlars – flourish.

Beyond the back garden is a tearoom; upstairs is the restaurant. Tea menus include traditional tarts using fruits from the garden, and from time to time there are special candle-lit suppers and lunches featuring old recipes such as Dame Alice Soup.

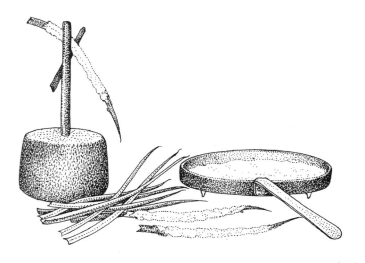

Dame Alice Soup

1 small onion, chopped
2 small carrots, chopped
50g (2oz) butter
1 bayleaf
5ml (1 teaspoon) celery seeds (these are essential)
5ml (1 teaspoon) fresh thyme
5ml (1 teaspoon) fresh parsley
6 peppercorns
50g (2oz) plain flour
675ml (1¼ pints) vegetable stock
250ml (½ pint) milk
salt and pepper
5ml (1 teaspoon) Marmite

Fry the chopped onion and carrots in the butter in a large saucepan for a minute or two. Add the bayleaf, celery seeds, thyme, parsley and peppercorns, and continue to cook to bring out the flavours of the herbs. Stir in the flour, add the stock and bring to the boil, stirring frequently. Simmer gently for 15 minutes. Pour in the milk, season with salt and pepper and stir in the Marmite. Bring almost to the boil and serve.

This is based on a very old recipe. Dame Alice Whitgreave was the mother of Thomas 'The Preserver' and helped to shelter Charles II in 1651.

Almondines

900g (2lb) potatoes
25g (1oz) butter
1 egg
10ml (1 dessertspoon) fresh chopped herbs
45ml (3 tablespoons) ground almonds
salt and pepper
115-170g (4-6oz) flaked almonds

Preheat oven: 190°C, 375°F; gas mark 5.

Peel the potatoes and chop them roughly. Cook them in salted water until tender, drain and mash with the butter. Add the egg, herbs and salt and pepper to taste. Form into small balls, about the size of small plums, and roll in the flaked almonds. Chill for about 30 minutes in the fridge.

Place the almond balls on a lightly greased baking sheet and bake in the preheated oven for 15-20 minutes until they are lightly golden.

Potato Nests

Make up the same potato mixture as for 'Almondines' above

Filling

225g (8oz) carrots, roughly chopped
1 clove of garlic, unpeeled

25g (1oz) butter
salt and pepper

Preheat oven: 180°C, 350°F; gas mark 4.

Pipe the potato mixture into nest shapes, 6·25cm (2½in) across, on a greased baking sheet and bake in the oven for 15 minutes.

Boil the carrots with the unpeeled garlic until cooked. Drain and pop the garlic out of its skin. Blend the carrots and garlic in a food processor with the butter until you have a purée. Season with salt and pepper. Put a spoonful of purée into each nest and put back in the oven for a further 10–15 minutes.

Alternative Fillings

Try the Spicy Tomato Topping from Castle Drogo (p.44). Substitute a good handful of chopped fresh basil for the chilli powder.

Spinach Tart with Three Cheeses

Pastry

170g (6oz) plain wholemeal flour
50g (2oz) plain white flour
pinch of salt

50g (2oz) butter
50g (2oz) vegetarian lard
30ml (2 tablespoons) cold water

Filling

1 medium onion, finely chopped
1 clove of garlic, crushed
25g (1oz) butter
450g (1lb) frozen spinach
2 eggs, lightly beaten

30ml (2 tablespoons) Parmesan
  cheese
225g (8oz) curd cheese
115g (4oz) Mozzarella cheese cut
  into little cubes

Preheat oven: 220°C, 425°F; gas mark 7.

Grease a 23cm (9in) loose-bottomed flan tin. In a large bowl mix together the flours and salt. Cut the fats into pieces, then using your fingers, rub the fats until the mixture resembles fine breadcrumbs. Add the water and gently gather the pastry together into a ball. Turn out on to a floured board and knead lightly, reserve a third then roll the rest out to the required size. Line the tin with the pastry and prick the base with a fork. Cook on a baking sheet in the centre of the oven until set for approximately 15 minutes.

Lower oven heat to: 180°C, 350°F; gas mark 4.

Sweat the onion and garlic with the butter until soft. Defrost, cook and drain well the spinach – cool slightly and stir in the onion and garlic together with the lightly beaten eggs. Add the three cheeses, season with salt and pepper and spoon into the pastry case.

Roll out the balance of the pastry and cut strips long enough to make a criss-cross pattern all over the surface of the tart. Brush the strips with milk and place the tart on the baking sheet in the oven. Bake for about 30–40 minutes.

Mulberry and Apple Plate Pie

Shortcrust Pastry

225g (8oz) plain flour	pinch of salt
50g (2oz) vegetarian lard	cold water to mix
50g (2oz) butter	

Filling

450g (1lb) cooking apples	75g (3oz) sugar
225g (8oz) mulberries	30ml (2 tablespoons) water

Preheat oven: 200°C, 400°F; gas mark 6.

Make up the pastry in the same method as Chirk Country Cheese Tart (p.58) and leave to rest.

Peel and slice the apples thinly into a saucepan together with the mulberries. Mix in the sugar and water and cook gently for about 10 minutes until the fruit is soft. Adjust the sweetness if necessary. Leave to cool.

Preheat the oven, put in a baking sheet and lightly grease a 25cm (10in) pie plate. Roll out a little more than half the pastry and line the plate, pressing it gently and firmly. Spoon in the cooled filling, then roll out the other half of the pastry to form a lid. Brush the bottom layer of pastry round the edge with water, then fix the pastry lid into place. Trim the edges and use any trimmings as decoration. Make a hole in the centre for the steam. Brush with milk and sprinkle on a dusting of caster sugar.

Place the pie on a baking sheet and bake for 30 minutes.

Tafferty Tart

350g (12oz) shortcrust pastry (using the amounts and method for Mulberry and Apple Plate Pie, above)

8 large cooking apples, thinly sliced

140g (5oz) sugar blended with the grated rind of 1 lemon and some of the lemon pulp, finely chopped

butter

Topping

115–170g (4–6oz) icing sugar

15ml (1 tablespoon) milk

15ml (1 tablespoon) lemon juice

Preheat oven: 200°C, 400°F; gas mark 6.

Grease a 25cm (10in) pie plate. Roll out over half of the pastry and line the plate, pressing it gently and firmly into place. Arrange the thinly sliced apples in layers, sprinkling each layer with the lemon and sugar mixture. Dot with butter and cover with the remainder of the pastry arranged in lattice strips. Place in the oven on a baking sheet and bake for 35 minutes.

While warm, drizzle with the topping made by mixing the ingredients together to produce a pouring consistency.

Quince Jam

900g (2lb) prepared quinces

1·4kg (3lb) sugar

juice of 1 lemon

water

Peel, core and chop the quinces into small pieces. Put them in a saucepan with enough water to cover and cook slowly until the fruit is really soft – this takes 20–30 minutes. Then add the sugar and lemon juice and stir until dissolved. Boil rapidly until setting point is reached. Leave to cool and then pot and cover in the usual way. Makes about 2·3kg (5lb).

Quinces ripen in October – when the leaves start to fall – and are even better if used after a frost.

Oxburgh Hall

The Bedingfeld family have always been both Royalists and Catholic. Oxburgh Hall has been their home for five hundred years and members of the family still live in part of this beautiful house. Their history is as much part of its fabric as the bricks and mortar of its mellow red walls.

It appears to be a castle with crenellated towers, a gatehouse and a moat, but although fifteenth-century Norfolk was turbulent, Oxburgh was not built to withstand siege and bombardment. It was a fortified manor appropriate for a gentleman of substance.

Through the centuries, the Bedingfelds served successive monarchs loyally in different roles. Some of these were extremely delicate. Sir Edmund Bedingfeld was steward to Catherine of Aragon after Henry VIII divorced her: his son Henry served Queen Mary Tudor by acting as jailer to her half-sister, the Princess Elizabeth. Luckily Elizabeth seemed to bear him no ill will, and visitors can still see an apparently amicable letter written to him by the Queen after her accession.

During the next three hundred years, the fortunes of the Bedingfelds fluctuated according to the current attitudes to their faith. As staunch Catholics, they endured persecution, heavy fines and restrictions. We can still see the entrance to a claustrophobic priest's hole, a reminder of those difficult years. However, most of the rooms visited now are the result of happier times. They are exuberantly Victorian, reflecting the relief that the Catholic Emancipation Act of 1829 brought. The walls glow with brightly coloured wallpapers and embossed leather; huge pieces of furniture incorporate medieval and contemporary carving. Now allowed a place of worship, the 6th Baronet, Sir Henry Paston-Bedingfeld, built in the grounds a chapel which is also full of colour and carvings celebrating the family's faith.

Appropriately for a house so full of history, historic recipes and traditional ingredients feature on the menu here. Pottage, made with meat or fish for the rich, vegetables for the less well off, was a staple of the medieval diet – and still a great favourite at Oxburgh.

Alison Sloan, who invents delicious modern versions of historic recipes for both Oxburgh and nearby Peckover House, has given me a superlative Vegetable and Nut Greate Pye, as well as other pies, tarts and a delicious colourful cheese pudding which also uses root vegetables which grow so well in the rich Norfolk soil.

Vegetable and Nut Greate Pye

225g (8oz) shortcrust pastry
¼ white cabbage, shredded, cooked and well drained
115g (4oz) sliced raw mushrooms
50g (2oz) vegetarian suet
50g (2oz) pine nuts or walnut pieces
25g (1oz) ground almonds
50g (2oz) chopped dates
½ teaspoon cinnamon
½ teaspoon nutmeg
50g (2oz) Parmesan cheese

Preheat oven: 180°C, 350°F; gas mark 4.

Line a 23cm (9in) flan tin with two thirds of the pastry. Prick the base and chill while you mix all the other ingredients together for the filling. Roll out the remainder of the pastry. Pile the filling into the tin – it should be fairly full – and cover with the pastry lid. Brush with milk or beaten egg to glaze. Bake approximately 35–40 minutes or until the pastry is golden. The juices from the raw mushrooms flavour the pie as they cook during baking.

Cheese Pudding

250 g (10 oz) soft white breadcrumbs
300 ml (½ pint) milk
200 g (7 oz) melted butter
170 g (6 oz) mature Cheddar grated
4 eggs, separated

50 g (2 oz) grated beetroot
50 g (2 oz) grated carrot
30 ml (2 tablespoons) fresh parsley,
   finely chopped

Preheat oven: 190°C, 375°F; gas mark 5.

Butter a 20 cm (8 in) china soufflé or gratin dish. Pour the milk onto the breadcrumbs in a bowl large enough to take all the ingredients. Stir in the melted butter and cheese and egg yolks, together with the grated beetroot and carrot. Whisk the egg whites until they are frothy (about 5 minutes) and fold them into the mixture together with the parsley. Pour the mixture into the buttered dish and bake approximately 20 minutes until firm and slightly golden.

At Oxburgh, this is served with a herb and lettuce salad and home-made chutney.

Cabbage and Cheese Pie

350 g (12 oz) puff pastry
¼ white cabbage
115 g (4 oz) mature Cheddar cheese
   grated

good pinch of fresh nutmeg
salt and pepper to taste
2 eggs
25 g (1 oz) melted butter

Preheat oven: 190°C, 375°F; gas mark 5.

Line a 23 cm (9 in) flan tin with half the pastry. Shred the cabbage finely, cook until *al dente* and drain well. While it is still hot, stir in the grated cheese, season with nutmeg, pepper and salt. Place in the pastry case. Beat the eggs with the butter and pour over the cabbage. Roll out the remaining pastry and place over the filling as a lid. Bake for about 30 minutes.

Spiced Bean Pottage

115g (4oz) chickpeas washed and
   soaked overnight
170g (6oz) dried haricot beans,
   washed and soaked overnight
90ml (6 tablespoons) oil, sunflower
   or olive
2 red onions, diced
2 cloves of garlic, peeled and finely
   chopped
5ml (1 teaspoon) of each of the
   following: ground coriander,
   turmeric, cumin

1 fresh chilli, de-seeded and finely
   chopped (optional, leave it out if
   you prefer a less 'hot' dish)
juice and rind of 1 lemon
2 red peppers diced
225g (8oz) spinach, washed, stalked
   and shredded
50g (2oz) pinenuts
salt and pepper to taste

NB: This recipe must be started the previous day.

Soak the beans and chickpeas overnight, drain.

Heat 75ml (5 tablespoons) of the oil and sauté the onions and garlic for a couple of minutes. Then add the spices and the chilli. Cook for a further 2–3 minutes and add the lemon juice and rind and the drained haricot beans and chickpeas. Cover with water, bring to the boil, cover the pan and simmer until the beans and peas are tender. This will take about three hours. Heat the remaining oil and fry the peppers until tender. Add to the mixture with the spinach and pinenuts. Season with salt and pepper to taste. Serve piping hot with lots of crusty bread.

Pottage was eaten by everyone in the Middle Ages. This modern version, adapted now by Alison and myself, was originally invented by Sara Paston-Williams who writes and lectures on historic food for the National Trust.

Petworth House

Petworth House is a jewel of a house in a setting as important as itself – Capability Brown's masterpiece. The great west front of the mansion, over 300 foot long, faces an extensive park and pleasure gardens with serpentine lakes, islands, temples, a folly, rare trees and shrubs, producing a feeling of spaciousness and serenity rare in the crowded south east. Deer graze beneath Brown's carefully placed clumps of trees, in the summer the park hosts picnics and impromptu cricket matches, on the horizon is a turreted Gothick folly, and in the winter – for the park is open all year – the fine views and clean air off the South Downs are enjoyed by visitors from afar and locals from the town.

This is peculiarly appropriate, since unusually for a 'country house' the cottages, shops and parish church of Petworth huddle right up against the east side of the house, home of the Percy and Wyndham families since 1150. The mansion is a treasure house of paintings, sculpture and carving, collected by the cultured earls of Northumberland and Egremont. The 9th Earl of Northumberland built up a fine library of books, many still at Petworth. After spending sixteen years in the Tower under suspicion of complicity in the Gunpowder Plot, he retired to Petworth to experiment in science and alchemy, earning the nickname of the 'Wizard Earl'. The 6th Duke of Somerset rebuilt the house in 1688, as we see it today, and the 2nd Earl of Egremont collected many of the old masters and antique statuary. Under the benign and humane influence of the 3rd Earl, who held the title for 65 years, Petworth enjoyed its 'golden age'. His hospitality was famous, 'the very animals at Petworth seemed happier than in any other spot on earth'. A great patron of all the arts, he numbered many writers and painters among his friends. Turner spent many years there painting glowing landscapes, some of which still hang in the North Gallery and the Turner Room. The Earl's consuming interest in agriculture led to the promotion of new methods to improve the lot of his tenants – a delightful picture in the North Gallery depicts a feast given by him at Petworth to cheer up his workers during a year of depression.

The North Gallery was his creation: on its dark tea-coloured walls are hung works by Turner, Gainsborough, Reynolds, Wilson and Romney and a host of less well-known painters. The 3rd Earl also formed the Carved Room in which cherubs, musical instruments, baskets of flowers, fruit, birds, palm trees, lobsters, crabs, sole and partridges, exquisitely carved in limewood by Grinling Gibbons, John Selden and Jonathan Ritson, tumble from ceiling to floor. Beyond the Carved Room is the Marble Hall and the Beauty Room, so-called because portraits of Queen Anne and her ladies-in-waiting line the walls.

Cross the lawn at the back of the house and you are in another world. These are the Servants' Quarters. Petworth had an army of servants, indoors and outdoors, each with a role to play in the smooth running of the estate. The rooms too were carefully planned, larders, dairies, food storage and service rooms culminating in the great kitchen. The kitchen, together with the pastry, the scullery, the larder and the chef's sitting-room have been carefully restored to their late nineteenth-century heyday. In the kitchen, cooking styles spanning 300 years can be seen, although the huge *batterie de cuisine*, copper pots and pans of every imaginable size and shape, may impress most. Between 100 and 400 meals a day were produced from this complex.

At the other end of the building is the huge Audit Room where farmers came to pay their dues. It is now the tea-room. Do take tea if you can – Petworth cakes are famous. For lunch you will find simple fare, carefully cooked: home-made soup, vegetable bakes served in individual pots and rich vegetable quiche flavoured with horseradish and herbs.

Petworth Vegetable Bakes

This will fill four individual gratin dishes

1 cauliflower
675g (1½lb) courgettes
37g (1½oz) butter
37g (1½oz) flour

400ml (¾ pint) milk
5ml (1 teaspoon) Dijon mustard
5ml (1 teaspoon) mixed herbs

Toppings
Either: 450g (1 lb) cooked, sliced new potatoes and a little melted butter

or: 450g (1 lb) swede, cooked and mashed until fluffy with butter, salt and lots of freshly ground black pepper

Preheat oven: 160°C, 325°F; gas mark 3.

Divide the cauliflower into florets and slice courgettes into 6mm (¼ inch) slices. Divide between the four dishes. Make a white sauce: melt the butter in a saucepan, stir in the flour and cook for a minute or two before pouring in the milk. Stirring all the time, bring to the boil, then add a teaspoon of Dijon mustard and one of mixed herbs. Pour over the dishes the white sauce, cover with either of the toppings and cook in the preheated oven for 20 minutes.

Vegetarian Quiche in Wholemeal Herb Pastry

Pastry

225g (8oz) plain wholemeal flour
10ml (1 dessertspoon) mixed herbs
pinch of salt

115g (4oz) hard margarine
cold water to mix

Filling

10ml (1 dessertspoon) sunflower oil
1 small onion, sliced
2 tomatoes, sliced
½ red pepper, sliced
½ green pepper, sliced
115g (4oz) mushrooms, sliced
2 courgettes, sliced
2 sticks of celery, sliced
or use any combination of these
   vegetables sufficient to fill
   the case

10ml (1 dessertspoon) creamed
   horseradish
10ml (1 dessertspoon) fresh basil
4 eggs
150ml (¼ pint) milk
150ml (¼ pint) cream
salt, pepper and Worcestershire
   sauce to taste

Topping

a handful of chopped hazelnuts and/or poppy-seeds

Preheat oven: 190°C, 375°F; gas mark 5.

Place flour, herbs and salt in bowl, rub in margarine with fingertips until the consistency of crunchy breadcrumbs and mix with enough water to form a stiff dough. Roll out on a floured board. Line a greased, fluted quiche dish with the pastry and brush with beaten egg on base and sides to give a crisp pastry.

To make the filling, cook sliced onion in vegetable oil and two teaspoons of water until soft but not brown. Add sliced tomatoes, red and green peppers, sliced mushrooms, courgettes and celery. Cook for 5 minutes stirring often. Add the horseradish sauce and the basil. Stir and cook for a few minutes until thick and creamy.

Beat four eggs into the milk and cream and add salt and pepper and a dash of Worcestershire sauce. Combine the cooked vegetables and egg mixture and pour into pastry case. Chop a handful of hazelnuts and sprinkle on top with poppy-seeds.

Place on a baking tray (most important to ensure that the bottom of pastry is properly cooked) in the middle of a preheated oven and cook for about 40 minutes.

Almond Topped Apricot Cake

Cake

170g (6oz) butter, softened
170g (6oz) caster sugar
3 eggs

170g (6oz) self-raising flour
75g (3oz) ground almonds
115g (4oz) apricots, chopped

Topping

50g (2oz) butter
50g (2oz) demerara sugar

5ml (1 level teaspoon) golden syrup
50g (2oz) flaked almonds

Preheat oven: 180°C, 350°F; gas mark 4.

Cream cake butter and sugar together until light, pale and fluffy. Gradually beat in the eggs, adding 15ml (one tablespoon) of flour with each egg. Finally fold in the remaining flour, ground almonds and apricots. Spoon into a 20cm (8in) spring clip tin which has been base lined and greased, and level the top. Bake for 45–50 minutes.

While the cake is baking, prepare the topping. Melt the butter, demerara sugar and syrup in a small pan. Heat very gently until the sugar dissolves. Stir in the almonds, spoon over the hot cake and return to the oven for 10–15 minutes to brown.

Apricots are credited with prolonging life and fertility, particularly in the Kashgar region of Pakistan where the fruit is grown in quantity and eaten as a staple part of the diet.

Eat the cake hot as a pudding with yoghurt, or cold for tea. Either way it's delicious.

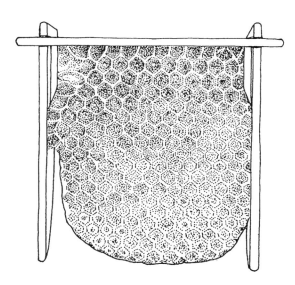

Sussex Apple Cake

225g (8oz) vegetarian margarine	225g (8oz) self-raising wholemeal flour
225g (8oz) dark brown soft sugar	2·5ml (½ teaspoon) ground cloves
3 eggs	400g (14oz) cooking apples, peeled and chopped
140g (5oz) walnuts	
140g (5oz) sultanas (or raisins)	

Preheat oven: 180°C, 350°F; gas mark 4.

Grease and base line a 20–23cm (8–9in) loose-bottomed tin. Cream together the margarine and 170g (6oz) of the sugar. Whip the eggs lightly and beat into the margarine and sugar. Combine 115g (4oz) of the crushed walnuts, the sultanas, flour, chopped apples (sliced in a processor or grated) and add cloves.

    Put half the cake mixture into the bottom of the tin, then a layer of the fruit and nut mixture and top with the rest of the cake mixture. Sprinkle the remaining 50g (2oz) of sugar and 25g (1oz) walnuts on top. Bake in oven for 1½ hours.

Iced Tea

Good quality Indian tea	Mint
Ice cubes	Lemon (or strawberries)

Make a pot of strong tea according to the number of glasses. Fill each glass with ice cubes, add two sprigs of mint and a slice of lemon to each glass – for special occasions sliced fresh strawberries look spectacular. Pour over the tea and serve.

    Very refreshing on a hot day.

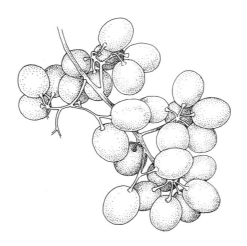

Quarry Bank Mill

The Industrial Revolution altered the face of Britain and the lives of millions of people. The huge changes caused by the rise of the great industries of the late eighteenth century – steel, coal and of course, cotton – are still affecting us today. Quarry Bank Cotton Mill at Styal, Cheshire, founded in 1784, was a pioneer factory site of that revolution.

We are apt to associate industry with grime and ugliness, but at Quarry Bank you will find the human face of the textile trade, set in handsome buildings in a naturally beautiful valley. A mill required power – before the ages of steam and electricity, water provided that power – so at Styal water power was harnessed with pool, weir and headrace from the River Bollin.

Styal is no dusty fusty museum. The experts and enthusiasts you will meet there will bring alive the history of textiles from the early days of spinning and weaving on a hand loom and into the great mechanical weaving sheds which continue to weave 100 per cent cotton calico today. The cloth is printed with designs exclusive to Styal. Full ranges of clothing, textile products and cloth by the metre are available in the mill shop.

The Greg family who founded Styal built up the business, presided during the great years and later struggled against the changes in demand and world markets. For two centuries, their lives were inextricably linked with Styal. Samuel Greg and his sons relied largely on poorhouse labour and founded Styal village to house the workforce. By 1790 an Apprentice House was built. Today, like the local schoolchildren, you can experience the hard lives of these 'parish' children. In the whitewashed house are the buckle beds, the desks, slates and pencils, the fustian uniforms, the porridge boiler, even the leeches and potions that the Superintendent used to dose the ailing boys and girls. Long hours, wages of a few shillings a week, crippling fines for misdemeanours, non-existent free time – it all seems draconian now but the Gregs considered themselves good employers by the standards of their time and were proud of their paternalistic labour relations.

You will find the restaurant at Styal in one of the old weaving sheds. No gluey, burnt apprentice porridge here, eat local specialities such as Pan Haggerty and enjoy the views towards the weir. The Quarry Bank Mill community is a living example of our industrial heritage.

Cucumber and Mint Salad

1 large cucumber, cubed
mint, chopped, to taste

140g (5oz) carton thick natural yoghurt

Wash and cut the cucumber into 2·5cm (1in) cubes and place in a decorative glass bowl. If using fresh mint, bruise the leaves and chop finely. If using concentrated mint from a jar, about 6ml (1 heaped teaspoon) should be sufficient. Stir the mint into the yoghurt, then pour over the cucumber and toss to combine. Cover and leave in the fridge for about 45 minutes for the flavours to marinate before serving.

Mixed Bean and Mandarin salad

1 medium tin red kidney beans
1 small tin mandarins in own juice

115g (4oz) cooked broad beans
salt and freshly ground black pepper

Thoroughly rinse the kidney beans and drain. Drain the juice from the mandarins and reserve. Combine the kidney beans, broad beans and mandarins in a salad bowl, season with a little salt and black pepper and toss lightly with a little of the mandarin juice.

Pan Haggerty

450g (1lb) potatoes
225g (8oz) onions
15ml (1 tablespoon) white Flora
 (or butter)

115g (4oz) Lancashire cheese,
 grated
salt and pepper

Slice the potatoes and onions very thinly. Heat the Flora in a large non-stick frying pan and put in the potatoes and onions with the grated cheese in layers, seasoning each layer lightly with salt and pepper. Fry it all gently until cooked. Place in an ovenproof casserole dish and brown under a grill. This makes a delicious supper dish served with a crisp, green salad.

Leek and Parsnip Bake

Makes four gratin dishes

15ml (1 tablespoon) vegetable oil	5ml (1 teaspoon) mustard
4 washed leeks, chopped into chunks	400ml (¾ pint) milk
450g (1 lb) parsnips, sliced	225g (8oz) cheese, grated
75g (3oz) butter	2 or 3 sticks of celery
50g (2oz) plain flour	flaked almonds

Preheat oven: 190°C, 375°F; gas mark 5.

Heat the oil gently in a large frying pan and sauté the leeks and parsnips until cooked but still slightly crunchy. Divide the vegetables evenly among 4 individual gratin dishes. Make a cheese sauce; melt the butter in a saucepan, stir in the flour with a teaspoon of mustard and cook for a minute or two before pouring in the milk. Stirring all the time, bring to the boil, then add 170g (6oz) of the grated cheese.

Pour the cheese sauce over the vegetables and mix lightly together to combine the ingredients. Slice the sticks of celery very thinly. Sprinkle the remaining grated cheese over each dish followed by the sliced celery and top with flaked almonds. Bake in the oven for 15 minutes until lightly golden on top.

Old Hannah's Cheshire Potato Cakes

8oz (225g) self-raising flour	8oz (225g) left-over mashed
½ teaspoon (2·5ml) salt	potatoes or fresh
2oz (50g) butter or margarine	1 egg, beaten
	a little milk if required

Preheat oven: 190°C, 375°F; gas mark 5.

Grease a baking tray. Place the flour and salt in a bowl with the fat. Rub the fat in the flour using your fingertips, then fork in the mashed potatoes.

Make a well in the centre of the mixture and drop in the beaten egg. Fork it into the mixture using a little milk if necessary, to give a soft pliable dough. Finish by kneading the dough with your hands until smooth. Roll it out to approximately 1·25cm (½in) thick and cut into rounds with a pastry cutter. Space them out on the prepared baking sheet and bake for 30 minutes.

Take out of the oven and wrap in a clean tea towel to keep them warm and soft. Split, butter and spread them with jam or syrup and serve while hot. Leftover cakes can be reheated, but they will have a crispy surface.

Orange Wholemeal Cake

115g (4oz) soft margarine	50g (2oz) wholemeal self-raising flour
115g (4oz) light soft brown sugar	½ level teaspoon baking powder
2 eggs	grated rind of 1 orange (the juice is used in the cake topping)
50g (2oz) white self-raising flour	

Topping

75g (3oz) sieved icing sugar	1 tablespoon of marmalade (not too chunky)
25g (1oz) soft margarine	juice of 1 orange

Preheat oven 180°C, 350°F; gas mark 4.

Line a 20cm (8in) cake tin.

Place all the cake ingredients in a bowl and beat well with an electric whisk until light and creamy. Place the mixture in the tin and level the top. Bake approximately 30–40 minutes until well risen and slightly shrunk from the sides of the tin. Leave approximately 15 minutes in the tin to cool. Turn out on to a wire rack and cool completely before topping the cake.

Beat all the ingredients of the topping together until soft enough to be spreadable. Top cake with mixture, sprinkle with orange zest or garnish with fresh orange slices just before serving if you wish.

Oat Biscuits

Makes approximately 20 biscuits

50g (2oz) caster sugar	115g (4oz) rolled oats
115g (4oz) soft margarine	50g (4oz) plain flour

Preheat oven: 180°C, 350°F; gas mark 4.

Line a baking sheet with baking parchment. Cream sugar and margarine together until light and fluffy. Fold in oats and flour and mix to a soft dough. Wrap in cling film and leave in the fridge for an hour or two to firm up. Roll out to approximately 5cm (2in) thickness on a lightly floured surface. Cut in 2cm (¾in) circles with a plain cutter and place on baking tray. Bake approximately 15 minutes until gold brown. When cool, move to a wire rack. These will keep for weeks in an airtight tin.

Banana Bread

115g (4oz) butter or soft margarine	6ml (1 heaped teaspoon) baking powder
115g (4oz) caster sugar	1·25ml (¼ teaspoon) bicarbonate of soda
225g (8oz) mashed bananas (overripe bananas are particularly suitable)	1·25ml (¼ teaspoon) salt
1 egg, lightly beaten	1·25ml (¼ teaspoon) vanilla essence
200g (7oz) plain flour	

Preheat oven: 180°C, 350°F; gas mark 4.

Grease and line a 450g (1lb) loaf tin.

Cream together the butter and sugar until light and fluffy. Stir in the mashed bananas and the beaten egg; do not worry if the mixture looks curdled at this stage.

Gradually fold in the sieved, dry ingredients and the vanilla essence. Spoon into the prepared loaf tin and bake for 45–50 minutes, until the cake springs back when lightly pressed.

Cool in the tin for 10 minutes before turning out on to a wire rack to cool completely.

Serve this loaf cake sliced thickly and buttered. It freezes well.

Styal Carrot Cake

170g (6oz) carrots, grated	170g (6oz) wholemeal flour
115g (4oz) walnuts	5ml (1 teaspoon) cinnamon
170g (6oz) soft brown sugar	5ml (1 teaspoon) bicarbonate of soda
170g (6oz) corn oil	
2 eggs, lightly beaten	

Topping

50g (2oz) soft margarine	75g (3oz) sifted icing sugar
170g (6oz) cream cheese	walnuts to decorate
rind ½ lemon, grated	

Preheat oven: 180°C, 350°F; gas mark 4.

Grease and bottom line a 20cm (8in) cake tin. Grate the washed and peeled carrots and finely chop the walnuts. Mix together in a basin with the soft brown sugar. Stir in the corn oil and the two beaten eggs and mix thoroughly together.

Stir together the wholemeal flour, cinnamon and bicarbonate of soda and fold these dry ingredients into the carrot mixture, lightly but thoroughly. Spoon into the prepared tin and bake for approximately 50 minutes. The cake is cooked when it springs back when lightly pressed with a finger. Leave to cool in the tin for a few minutes, then turn out on to a wire rack.

Make the topping by creaming together the margarine and cream cheese until light and fluffy. Stir the lemon rind into the icing sugar and gradually beat this into the creamed mixture until all the sugar is incorporated.

When the cake is cold, spread the topping over the top of the cake and decorate with chopped walnuts. Store in the fridge.

Dr Peter Holland was doctor to the apprentices at Styal from 1795 to 1837, and the Mill still has his notebooks. The apprentices were healthy by the standards of their time. Samuel Greg ensured this by insisting that any children supplied to him by parish authorities should come on a trial period of a month 'to ascertain their probable healthiness'. In practice, the system was more relaxed. Notes for 28 February 1833 state: 'Sarah Powell, Liverpool, aged 9. Healthy now. Had inflamed eyes a year ago but they are well now, and there does not seem any objection to engaging her.'

Many of the health problems were work-related sore eyes, headaches, cuts, bruises. Accidents were not often recorded.

Dr Holland's 'science' consisted of four humours medicine – bad body fluid caused any number of infections and health problems. Leeches were used to take away bad blood. For instance, Elizabeth Bracegirdle was treated for inflamed eyes in November 1841: 'four leeches round the right eye and in three days a blister behind the right ear, to be repeated in five or six days.'

Here are some interesting facts about leeches generously supplied by the Apprentice House: each leech has 300 teeth and 3 jaws; a leech can take 225 ml (8 fl oz) blood (if the doctor snipped the tail, it would take more, but it would also die); they can gorge feed every six months. In 1830, the leeches for Styal probably came from the River Bollin, but leech gatherers also collected them from the Lake District. Doctors could 'drain' leeches by putting them in a bowl of hot water and pressing the blood out of them. Leeches are being used again in hospitals to aid micro-surgery.

Rufford Old Hall

The only part of the sixteenth-century manor house at Rufford to survive in original form faces visitors coming up the drive. The Great Hall remains the main glory of the house, built on the strength of a series of marriages between the Heskeths and local heiresses. The debt is recorded in the roof bosses of the Great Hall which display the arms of the Lancashire families with which the Heskeths were intermarried, and its elaborate hammer-beam roof supports the stone slates with which the whole house is covered. Below is what is described as a moveable screen, though its size and three finials that almost double its height make it appear anything but portable. It is one of only three remaining in England. The site of the high table, from the time when all members of a household irrespective of rank dined together, is indicated by a canopy of honour and by a great bay window that looks north.

Connecting the Great Hall with a brick Carolean wing is a castellated tower built in 1821 that looms over the earlier parts. The wings incorporates the medieval east wing and its rooms include a large drawing-room with a spy-hole into the Great Hall.

Spread round the house you will find the Philip Ashcroft Collection, everyday items from the nineteenth century. Mr Ashcroft was a member of an old village family still living in Rufford and the first curator of Rufford Old Hall. His collection gives a fascinating insight into the lives of ordinary Lancashire families. There are carefully worked samplers in the schoolroom, cow creamers, mugs and plates in the tea-rooms, and in the stables are the larger items – amongst them an enormous cheese press, an early water softener, a frightening man-trap, a towering penny-farthing and a genuine 'boneshaker' bicycle. Exercise was tough stuff. There are bats and bees in the roof. You may catch a glimpse of the even rarer red squirrel in the beautifully laid out gardens.

Home-made lunches and teas are served in two delightful small tearooms with stone flags, oak furniture and blue-and-white china and linen. Polished pewter and interesting storage jars line the walls, and on chilly days a cheerful fire crackles in the black-leaded range. Rufford lies on the flat fertile Lancashire plain, a great area for farming and market gardening. Maureen Dodsworth's recipes reflect the ingredients grown locally, principally vegetables and particularly potatoes, which are famously good in this district. Good 'ribsticking' food to sustain outdoor folk.

Leek and Potato Hot Pot

Makes four individual earthenware dishes

15 ml (1 tablespoon) sunflower oil
450 g (1 lb) leeks
40 g (1½ oz) butter
25 g (1 oz) plain flour
250 ml (½ pint) milk

5 ml (1 teaspoon) mustard
170 g (6oz) Cheddar cheese, grated
450 g (1 lb) new potatoes, cooked
parsley, chopped into 2·5 cm (1 in) pieces

Preheat oven: 160°C, 325°F; gas mark 3.

Trim, slice and wash leeks in a colander. Sauté gently in sunflower oil until soft but not mushy. Make a cheese sauce: melt the butter, and stir in and cook the flour for a couple of minutes. Gradually add the milk, stirring all the time, until the mixture comes to the boil and a thick sauce is made. Add the mustard and cheese and heat gently until melted into the sauce.

Arrange half the potatoes in the bottom of each dish, then the leeks, then cover with the cheese sauce. Arrange the balance of the potatoes on top, brush with a little extra oil and bake uncovered in the oven for 20 minutes. Serve with a scattering of chopped parsley.

Cabbage and Potato Hot Pot

450g (1 lb) Savoy cabbage
450g (1 lb) potatoes
2 large onions
115g (4oz) butter or margarine

5ml (1 teaspoon) mixed herbs
5ml (1 teaspoon) ground nutmeg
salt and pepper

Preheat oven: 220°C, 425°F; gas mark 7.

Slice cabbage and bring to the boil in boiling salted water. Drain in a colander. Peel potatoes and cut into 6mm (¼in) slices. Cook for 5 minutes in boiling water and drain. Slice onions and fry gently in half the butter or margarine until soft but not coloured. Arrange the vegetables in layers in an earthenware dish, seasoning each one with herbs, nutmeg, salt and pepper. Finish with a layer of potatoes. Dot with the remaining butter and bake in the oven for 30 minutes.

Garlic Roast Potatoes

1 large potato per person
115g (4oz) butter
2 cloves of garlic

15ml (1 tablespoon) of fresh parsley, chopped
15ml (1 tablespoon) mixed dried herbs

Preheat oven: 160°C, 325°F; gas mark 3.

To make the garlic butter, blend the butter, garlic, fresh parsley and mixed dried herbs. This is easily done in a food processor, but you can manage perfectly well with a fork if the butter is soft.

Peel the potatoes, slice in 6mm (¼in) slices almost through to the base. Melt the garlic butter. Stand each potato on an individual piece of foil large enough to wrap it in. Pour a little butter over each potato, using 25g (1oz) garlic butter per person, wrap it in foil and bake for 1 hour.

As well as the wonderful aroma when you unwrap them, you should be able to fan them out, which looks very attractive.

Vegetable Cobbler

3 medium carrots, peeled and sliced
½ small cauliflower, separated into
   florets
75g (3oz) margarine
8 small leeks, thickly sliced
2 small heads of fennel, sliced

25g (1oz) wholewheat flour
400ml (¾ pint) vegetable stock
salt and pepper
30ml (2 tablespoons) fresh parsley,
   chopped

Topping

225g (8oz) self-raising flour
5ml (1 teaspoon) mixed herbs
5ml (1 teaspoon) mustard powder
salt and pepper

50g (2oz) vegetarian lard
1 egg
milk to mix
75g (3oz) cheese, grated

Preheat oven: 180°C, 350°F; gas mark 4.

Cook carrots and cauliflower for 5 minutes in boiling, salted water and then drain. Place in an ovenproof dish. Melt half the margarine and fry the leeks and fennel over a moderate heat for 3–4 minutes. Add to casserole. Melt the rest of the margarine in a small saucepan, add the wholewheat flour and cook gently for a few minutes. Gradually add the vegetable stock and season if necessary. Simmer for a minute or two, add the parsley and pour over the vegetables. Cover the casserole and bake for 30 minutes.

To make the topping, sieve the flour with the mixed herbs, mustard powder and salt and pepper. Rub in the lard until the mixture resembles coarse breadcrumbs. Mix the egg with a little milk and combine to make a springy dough. Roll out to about 2cm (¾in) thick and cut into round scones with a biscuit cutter. Arrange scones on top of the vegetables round the edge of the casserole, sprinkle with the grated cheese. Increase the oven heat to 230°C, 450°F; gas mark 8 and bake the casserole for a further 15 minutes. Serve at once.

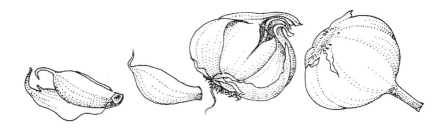

Celery and Cashew Nut Risotto

30ml (2 tablespoons) olive oil or sunflower oil	15ml (1 tablespoon) tomato purée
1 onion, finely sliced	170g (6oz) cashew nuts
4 large sticks of celery, chopped	bunch of spring onions, chopped
1 red pepper, diced	15ml (1 tablespoon) of fresh parsley, chopped
225g (8oz) brown rice	30ml (2 tablespoons) of Parmesan cheese, grated
500ml (1 pint) vegetable stock	
10ml (1 dessertspoon) oregano	

Sauté the chopped onion and celery in the oil in a large frying pan or wok until soft but not brown. Add the red pepper and the rice and stir well so that the rice is well coated with oil. Heat the stock in a small pan, pour one half over the rice mixture and add the oregano and tomato purée. Cover the pan with a lid or foil and simmer until the stock is almost absorbed. Then add the next half together with the cashew nuts and spring onions. Recover pan and simmer until the rice is tender. (You may need to top up with a little more stock.) It is important to stir the risotto frequently to ensure that is cooked throughout. Serve with parsley and cheese scattered over the top.

Olive oil and fresh Parmesan make this a luxurious dish.

Courgette and Tomato Bake

900g (2lb) courgettes	2 eggs
400g (14oz) tin chopped tomatoes	250ml (½ pint) milk
5ml (1 teaspoon) mixed herbs	salt and pepper to taste

Preheat oven: 180°C, 350°F; gas mark 4.

Wash, trim and slice the courgettes. Cook for 5 minutes until not quite tender in boiling water. Drain and layer in the bottom of an ovenproof dish, cover with the chopped tomatoes and herbs and season with pepper and salt. Lightly beat the eggs with the milk, pour over the tomatoes and set the dish uncovered in a roasting tin with water to come half way up the dish. Bake in the oven for about 30 to 40 minutes, until custard is firm.

Braised Red Cabbage

675–900g (1½ to 2lb) red cabbage
50g (2oz) butter
1 medium-sized onion, sliced
1 large cooking apple
150ml (¼ pint) cheap red wine, or stock
10ml (1 dessertspoon) salt

15ml (1 tablespoon) vinegar
2ml (½ level teaspoon) powdered cloves
2·5ml (½ teaspoon) grated nutmeg
freshly ground black pepper, to taste
15ml (1 level tablespoon) soft brown sugar

Remove the cabbage's outer leaves, white root and larger pieces of white pith, cut into quarters and shred finely. Place in a large bowl and cover with water. Drain after a minute.

Soften the onions in the melted butter in a large heavy pan, but do not brown. Peel, core and thickly slice the apple, and add to the pan with the wine or stock, salt, vinegar, cloves, nutmeg, plenty of black pepper and finally the cabbage. Combine and cover the pan tightly. Cook gently, stirring occasionally, for about 1 hour, until soft but not mushy. Stir in the sugar and serve.

This loses none of its flavour if reheated the following day.

Winter Sprout Salad

450g (1 lb) Brussel sprouts, finely shredded
225g (½lb) carrots, grated

½ small head of celery, chopped
75g (3oz) walnuts, broken

Dressing
1 small pot of yoghurt
150ml (¼ pint) mayonnaise

5ml (1 teaspoon) seedy mustard
salt and pepper to taste

Combine separately the ingredients of the salad and the dressing. Pour the dressing over the salad. Colourful and crunchy.

Wholemeal and Yoghurt Scones

450g (1lb) wholemeal flour
5ml (1 teaspoon) baking powder
50g (2oz) sugar
115g (4oz) sultanas

75g (3oz) margarine
225ml (8oz) natural yoghurt
(small pot)

Preheat oven: 220°C, 425°F; gas mark 7.

Sieve the flour and combine with the baking powder, sugar and sultanas. Rub in the fat, bind with the yoghurt and cut into rounds. Brush top with yoghurt and bake in the oven.

Health and Diet

The construction of railways throughout Britain did more to unify diet and the prices of food than any other development before the twentieth century. Until towns were linked with the rural hinterland, a poor harvest in one area could mean hunger and high prices even if other parts of the country had enjoyed good yields. Equally the labouring classes in some regions subsisted on food that is now known to be lacking in nutritional value or of limited help in preventing degenerative diseases. For example, the staple diet of the poor in the Midlands and the South was bread, cheese and potatoes washed down with tea, whereas the barley- or oat-based diet of those in Wales and the North was much healthier.

The penchant amongst the wealthy for rich food, meat and alcohol and too few fresh vegetables made gout, heart attacks and cirrhosis of the liver common ailments. Moreover, the risk of illness from food was compounded by methods of cooking and food preservation: brass and copper pans might combine with acid foods to produce poisonous verdigris, and the failure to boil preserved food in earthenware or glass jars could cause botulism. The difficulty of keeping food often meant that ingredients which would today be thrown out as bad were 'rescued' by dubious recipes.

Standen

Philip Webb, architect of Standen is quoted as saying: 'I am never satisfied with a design until it begins to look commonplace.' For 'commonplace' read 'a pleasant, commodious, stone Victorian house, beautifully positioned facing south on the North Downs, surrounded by informal gardens and with magnificent views across the River Medway to Ashdown Forest.'

Webb built the house in 1891 for James Beale, a successful solicitor, and his wife Margaret, who wanted a country house for weekends and holidays with their large family. The light airy rooms still convey this relaxed harmonious atmosphere, in total contrast to the cluttered dark rooms normally associated with Victorian interiors.

William Morris, the great nineteenth-century reformer of the decorative arts, was a lifelong friend of Webb, and Morris carpets, wallpapers and fabrics enrich many of the rooms. There is even furniture designed by Morris & Co., such as the seat furniture and the cabinet in the Drawing Room. In other rooms hang original Morris wallpapers and fabrics, now a little faded in contrast with modern copies of original designs that are still on sale today. You will find other great names in the Arts & Crafts Movement represented here: glowing, bold pots in red lustre ware by William de Morgan; Della Robbia pottery; furniture designed by the Misses Garrett; copperware and pottery by John Pearson; elegant electric light fittings by W. A. S. Benson; brass beds from the fashionable

Messrs Heal & Co.; and, of course, various items from the equally fashionable and innovative Messrs Liberty, who are still selling Mr Morris's fabric and wallpaper designs.

Wandering through these rooms and the unpretentious pleasant garden with its lovely views, it is easy to imagine the large Beale family, children, grandchildren and friends enjoying each others' company with conversation and games of billiards inside, promenades and croquet outside. Now Standen invites today's visitors to slow down a little and enjoy the experience of visiting a house and garden which exude the atmosphere of a slower, more leisured age. Standen must have been a pleasure then – it certainly is now.

Turn sharp left by the gate and you will find yourself in a fine old timber-framed barn. Home-made soups, vegetarian dishes and good cakes are on the menu. A previous manageress, Mrs Simons, gave me the recipe for Standen's Golden Cake. 'I tried to make the visitors feel they were coming to have lunch or tea with me personally.' Philip Webb and the Beales, I am sure, would have approved.

Lettuce Soup

15 ml (1 tablespoon) oil
25 g (1 oz) butter
350 g (12 oz) lettuce leaves
1 large leek, sliced

2 medium potatoes, peeled and
  chopped
500 ml (1 pint) vegetable stock
salt and freshly ground black pepper
parsley, chopped to decorate

Heat the oil and butter in a large saucepan. Tear the lettuce leaves into pieces and sauté in the pan with the sliced leek and chopped potatoes. Pour in the stock, bring to the boil and simmer until the vegetables are tender. Cool slightly before placing in a food processor and processing until smooth. Return to the saucepan and season to taste with salt and pepper. Reheat before serving, ladle into individual bowls and sprinkle over the fresh, chopped parsley.

If you have a row of 'bolting' lettuces (lettuces that are going to seed), this is an excellent recipe to make use of them.

Parsnip, Paprika and Mustard Soup

450 g (1 lb) parsnips
1 medium leek
1 tablespoon oil
25 g (1 oz) butter
1 heaped teaspoon paprika

1·25 litres (2 pints) vegetable stock
1 tablespoon Dijon mustard
1 teaspoon sugar
salt and pepper to taste

Peel and dice the parsnips, wash and dice the leek. Heat the oil and butter together in a pan large enough to take all the ingredients. Sauté the diced leek and parsnips for five minutes. Add the paprika, stir well to coat the vegetables and cook for a couple of minutes more. Add the vegetable stock, bring to the boil and simmer until the vegetables are soft. This takes approximately 20 minutes. Liquidise the mixture; return to the pan and stir in the mustard and sugar. Adjust seasoning, reheat until very hot and serve immediately with warm buttered bread rolls.

This soup has a lovely colour and a sophisticated flavour. If you can use smoked paprika – even better.

Leek Soufflé

450g (1 lb) leeks, washed and cut into rings	ground black pepper
	3 large eggs, separated
25g (1 oz) butter	

Sauce

25g (1 oz) butter	1·25ml (¼ teaspoon) grated nutmeg
25g (1 oz) flour	salt and pepper
250ml (½ pint) milk	75g (3oz) grated Gruyère cheese

Preheat oven: 190°C, 375°F; gas mark 5.

Grease a 1·25 litres (2 pint) soufflé dish.

Simmer the leeks in a little boiling water for a few minutes. Drain, add the butter and season.

For the sauce, melt the butter in a saucepan and stir in the flour. Gradually add the milk and bring to the boil, stirring continuously until the sauce thickens. Season with the grated nutmeg and salt and pepper, then stir in the Gruyère cheese.

Stir in the leeks and egg yolks. Whisk the egg whites until stiff and, with a large metal spoon, gently fold them into the soufflé mixture. Pour into the greased soufflé dish and bake for 40–50 minutes until well risen and golden. Serve immediately.

As a main course this serves 3–4, it could also be served as a starter by dividing the mixture between six little ramekins, well-buttered, and baking for 15–20 minutes.

Standen Golden Cake

225g (8oz) butter or margarine	225g (8oz) wholemeal self-raising flour
225g (8oz) caster sugar	
3 eggs	115g (4oz) sultanas
225g (8oz) carrots, grated	75ml (3fl oz) milk

Preheat oven: 180°C, 350°F; gas mark 4.

Grease and double base line a 20cm (8in) cake tin.

Cream together the butter and caster sugar until light and fluffy. Gradually beat in the eggs to the creamed mixture. Stir in the carrots, flour, sultanas and milk, making sure you mix the ingredients well together. Spoon into the prepared tin and bake for 60–70 minutes. Cool in the tin before turning out.

Mrs Simon's Golden Cake was justly famous amongst her customers.

Raisin and Bran Loaf

2 teacups All Bran	2 teacups milk
2 teacups dark brown sugar	2 teacups self-raising wholemeal
2 teacups raisins	flour

Place the All Bran cereal, sugar, raisins and milk into a pan. Stir, cover and leave overnight.

Preheat oven: 180°C, 350°F; gas mark 4.

Grease and bottom line a 900g (2lb) loaf tin.

Add the flour to the mixture; if too stiff, pour in a little more milk or milk and water, to make a soft consistency. Place in the prepared loaf tin and bake in the oven for 45–60 minutes, until a skewer comes out clean. Allow to cool for a few minutes before turning out and removing the lining paper.

Slice and serve spread with butter. A simple but good addition to a high-fibre diet.

Julie's Walnut Cookies

225g (8oz) butter or margarine	2 eggs
225g (8oz) soft brown sugar	115g (4oz) chopped walnuts
63g (2½oz) porridge oats	115g (4oz) chopped glacé cherries
140g (5oz) self-raising flour	1·25ml (¼ teaspoon) cinnamon

Preheat oven: 180°C, 350°F; gas mark 4.

Grease and line the base of a large Swiss roll tin or smooth-bottomed roasting tin.

Melt the butter in a large saucepan, add the sugar and cook gently until syrupy. Take off the heat and mix in all the other ingredients. Spread evenly over the base of the tin and bake for about 30 minutes.

Take out of the oven and cut into fingers. Leave to cool in the tin.

Wallington

Drive north east across the bleak, beautiful Northumbrian moors from Newcastle and suddenly, over the brow of a hill, Wallington appears below, a grey Palladian mansion, approached across a handsome bridge and guarded by four huge stone griffins' heads. (They once adorned one of the entrances to the City of London, Bishopsgate.)

Since 1688 Wallington has belonged first to the Blackett and later the Trevelyan families. Both had a tradition of public service. Throughout the centuries, Blacketts and Trevelyans served as Mayors of Newcastle and Members of Parliament. Although permanently short of money, Walter Calverley Blackett, whose portrait by Reynolds hangs in the Saloon, remodelled the house, built the stable block and created a beautiful walled valley garden, reached by a walk through woods that he planted.

All the Trevelyans were cultured and well read: in the well-stocked library you will find books annotated with amusingly barbed hand-written comments. They were also historians – Lord Macaulay, whose desk is in the house, was related by marriage – and dedicated to social reform. This was particularly true of Walter and Pauline Trevelyan, Victorian owners of Wallington. Walter was very interested in natural history, agriculture and the temperance movement: his signature, with Pauline's, appears on a tract against 'ardent spirits' in the Common Room. Pauline was deeply involved with the Pre-Raphaelite brotherhood, and was herself a talented painter. With a little help from John Ruskin, she and William Bell Scott created the huge allegorical pictures of Northumbrian history in the central hall. Although committed teetotallers – there are no public houses still on the Wallington estate – Pauline did persuade Walter to relax a little as far as house guests were concerned and table wine of doubtful quality was provided. One house guest, however, was not to be mollified by this gesture: Augustus Hare,

who stayed at Wallington in 1861 and 1862. On his first visit he arrived for lunch 'which was as peculiar as everything else (Lady Trevelyan and her artists feeding solely on artichokes and cauliflowers)'. On his second visit he sourly described the house 'like a great desert with one or two oases', though he ended up enjoying himself because of the excellent conversation of his hosts. Life with Walter and Pauline must have been interesting but uncomfortable.

Now things are ordered better. Allow time to see the elegant eighteenth-century interiors, the fine porcelain collection, a village of doll's-houses, and armies of lead soldiers and the Victorian kitchen. Upstairs is a pretty nursery, bedrooms full of family pictures and furniture and Lady Wilson's Cabinet of Curiosities – a room of glass cases, with the strangest mixture of objects: stuffed birds, eggs and minerals jostle with models, utensils, photographs and ephemera, designed to startle, intrigue and amaze the beholder.

Walk the woods, stroll in the sheltered valley garden and cross the grassy quadrangle to eat hearty Northumbrian food in the beamed Clocktower Restaurant. Northumbrians are proud of their leeks, and the soup and pudding given here would keep out the chill of the coldest winter day. Home-made biscuits are another speciality, easy to make and a treat to eat.

This notice hangs in the room containing the doll's-houses at Wallington:

Association for the Suppression of Intemperance

We the subscribers agree, so long as we belong to this Association, to abstain from the use of ardent spirits except for medicinal purposes, and to refrain from providing them for persons in our employ.

Signed by amongst others John Trevelyan
Pauline Trevelyan
Arthur Trevelyan
W. C. Trevelyan, all of Wallington

1831–34

Leek and Tarragon Soup

30 ml (2 tablespoons) oil
1 onion, peeled and chopped
450 g (1 lb) leeks, washed and finely sliced
1 carrot, peeled and chopped

15 ml (1 tablespoon) fresh tarragon leaves or 5 ml (1 teaspoon) dried tarragon
750 ml (1½ pints) vegetable stock (use the recipe on p.23 or two vegetable stock cubes)
salt and pepper to taste

To finish: a few more fresh tarragon leaves

Sauté the onions in the oil for five minutes. Add the leeks and carrot and cook gently for a further 10 minutes. Add the tarragon, fresh or dried, and cook a further five minutes. Add the stock, bring to the boil then simmer for about 25 minutes. Liquidise the mixture. Reheat to just below boiling and serve with fresh tarragon leaves on the top as a garnish.

A Northumberland cheese and herb scone is a good accompaniment to this tasty soup.

Leek, Cheese Bread and Butter Pudding

30 ml (2 tablespoons) vegetable oil
4 medium leeks, trimmed, washed and finely sliced
8 slices herb flavoured bread, sliced and buttered (If unavailable add 5 ml (1 teaspoon) dried mixed herbs to the leeks when sautéing)
6 eggs, well beaten
500 ml (1 pint) milk
300 ml (10 fl oz) double cream
15 ml (1 tablespoon) finely chopped fresh chives (use chive flowers when in season)
225 g (½ lb) Northumberland cheese, grated
salt and pepper to taste

Preheat oven: 180°C, 350°F; gas mark 4.

Butter a large ovenproof dish. Heat the oil, gently sauté the leeks until soft. Lay the bread in the dish interspersed with the softened leeks. Whisk together the eggs, milk and cream, stir the chives and grated cheese into the mixture and season to taste. Bake for approximately 50 minutes until golden and set but still wobbly in the middle.

Serve at once with a green salad. Local ingredients in a dish that is both tasty and lovely to look at.

Northumberland Cheese and Herb Scones

50 g (2 oz) margarine
450 g (1 lb) self-raising flour
225 g (8 oz) Northumberland cheese, grated
50 g (2 oz) Parmesan cheese, grated
3 ml (½ teaspoon) dried mixed herbs
10 ml (2 teaspoons) baking powder
1 egg
250 ml (½ pint) milk

Preheat oven: 200°C, 400°F; gas mark 6.

Rub margarine into flour. Stir in the cheeses, herbs and baking powder. Whisk the egg into the milk and use the mixture to bind the other ingredients to make a soft dough. Knead and roll out to about 1·25 cm (½ in) thickness. Cut into rounds with an 8 cm (3 in) cutter. Line a baking sheet with baking parchment, lay the scones on the parchment and bake approximately 10–15 minutes until brown and well risen.

Northumbrian Ginger Biscuits

170 g (6 oz) margarine
170 g (6 oz) sugar
15 ml (1 tablespoon) golden syrup

350 g (12 oz) plain flour sifted with
10 ml (2 teaspoons) each of
bicarbonate of soda, ginger
and cinnamon

Preheat oven: 160°C, 325°F; gas mark 3.

Line a baking sheet with baking parchment. Melt margarine, sugar and golden syrup in a saucepan. Add the flour, bicarbonate of soda, ginger and cinnamon and mix well. Roll small amounts of the mixture in your hands to form balls, approximately the size of a large walnut. Place these well apart on the baking sheet and flatten the top slightly of each one. Bake approximately 10–15 minutes until golden. Transfer to a wire tray to cool. These will keep for weeks in an airtight tin.

Wimpole Hall

Wimpole, the largest house in Cambridgeshire, is set with church, stables and home farm in a great park of mature trees, lakes, avenues and statuary. A romantic Gothick tower ruin, built in 1768 by Capability Brown, enhances the view from the house. Brown was only one of the celebrated architects and landscape gardeners who 'altered and improved' Sir Thomas Chicheley's original designs. James Gibbs, Charles Bridgeman, Henry Flitcroft, Sir John Soane, Humphry Repton and H. E. Kendall all contributed too. Today their achievement is an astonishingly harmonious blend of buildings and landscape.

Cambridgeshire is a countryside of gently rolling fields, tall trees and huge skies. Views are on the grand scale and so is Wimpole. Although the interiors are appropriately imposing, they are not overpowering. The last private owner of the house, Elsie Bambridge, Rudyard Kipling's daughter, died as recently as 1976. During her time at Wimpole, she furnished and decorated the house, filling it with pictures; her love and concern remains a strong influence. Through the tall windows the clear East Anglian light reflects fine carving, plasterwork and gilding, and illuminated, elegant, unfussy rooms. To me, the most beautiful of all is Sir John Soane's Yellow Drawing Room, lit from a painted dome, a wonderfully appropriate setting for the grand occasions of eighteenth-century country life. He also built a plunge bath where jaded gentry dipped for cleanliness rather than health!

James Gibbs' magnificent Baroque chapel inside the house may have been built as a suitable setting for performances by the orchestra kept by the then owner of Wimpole, Lord Harley. In complete contrast is the Wimpole parish church of St Andrew's, small and intimate, and full of marble monuments to the Yorke family* who owned Wimpole for over a hundred years. Beyond the church is H. E. Kendall's Victorian stables where a wagon ride can be taken to Sir John Soane's other contribution to Wimpole, the Home Farm buildings. Here the Rare Breeds Survival Trust is raising old strains of cattle, sheep, goats and other livestock, providing not only an opportunity to see these animals but also to make a positive contribution to farm-stock breeding in the future.

The extensive walled gardens are being brought back into production: three tons of potatoes, a ton of runner beans and 350 lbs of rhubarb are produced annually, much of which can be sampled in the restaurant. Now Sir John Soane's magnificent eighteenth-century greenhouses are also being restored, and once completed, the main glasshouse will provide salad crops.

Feast in style at Wimpole, below the chandeliers and gilded plasterwork of the original Great Dining Room. Splendid views across the park enhance the fresh delicious dishes. The recipes which follow, are all new to this edition. The high standard looks set to continue. Keith Goodwin, the current chef at Wimpole who gave me these recipes, says his greatest pleasure now, after many years cooking, is to train the next generation. I'm sure visitors to Wimpole over the years to come will benefit from his enthusiasm.

*The Yorke family at Erddig was related, pp.74–5.

Pickled Walnuts

Gather them before the shells begin to form, pick off the stalks and put them into a jar. Boil some good vinegar with a little salt and horseradish, some bruised pepper, ginger and cloves and pour it hot upon the bladder and let them stand a year. When the walnuts are all used, the vinegar may be improved and made useful for fish sauce and hashes, by boiling it up with anchovies, cloves and garlic; then strain it and cork it up in bottles.

The Housekeeper's Receipt Book 1813

Mushroom Soup

170g (6oz) butter
1 medium onion, finely chopped
450g (1lb) closed cup mushrooms,
  roughly chopped

170g (6oz) plain flour
1 litre (1¾ pints) milk

Sauté the chopped onion and mushrooms in half the butter for about five minutes. In a separate pan, melt the rest of the butter, stir in the flour and cook for a minute or two before pouring in the milk to make a sauce. At this point you have a choice. You can either first liquidise the mushroom mixture and then combine it with the white sauce. This will give you a smooth thick mushroom soup. If you prefer a chunky texture, simply combine the mushroom mixture and the white sauce. In either case, season to taste with salt and pepper, reheat the soup to just below boiling and serve immediately.

Pickled Walnut, Cheese and Red Onion Tartlets

225g (½lb) shortcrust pastry
  (use the recipe on p.58, but add
  5ml (1teaspoon) wholegrain
  mustard and a little water)
15ml (1 tablespoon) vegetable oil
1 large or 2 small red onions
  peeled and sliced

170g (6oz) cream cheese
170g (6oz) pickled walnuts, drained
  and chopped
3 eggs, beaten
150ml (¼ pint) double cream
salt and pepper to taste

Preheat oven: 180°C, 350°F; gas mark 4.

Roll out pastry and cut into large rounds to line individual tartlet tins. Prick the base of each tart and bake for approximately 10 minutes. Sauté the onions in the oil for three minutes. Set aside. Mix cream cheese and walnuts and divide the mixture amongst the tins. Whisk the eggs with the cream until thick and creamy, season with salt and pepper and pour over the cream cheese mixture. Scatter the sautéed onions on top and bake for about 15 minutes until puffed up and golden. Serve hot.

Wimpole has the National Walnut Collection, so this recipe is particularly appropriate.

Vegetable Pouches

Choux Pastry

300 ml (½ pint) water
115 g (4 oz) butter, chopped into
   small pieces

170 g (6 oz) plain flour sifted with a
   pinch of salt
3 medium eggs

Vegetable Filling

15 ml (1 tablespoon) vegetable oil
1 small onion, peeled and chopped
225 g (8 oz) courgettes, diced
115 g (4 oz) aubergines, diced
1 yellow pepper, depipped and diced

250 g (½ lb) chopped tomatoes
15 ml (1 tablespoon) tomato purée
a few chopped basil leaves
salt and pepper to taste

Preheat oven: 180°C, 350°F; gas mark 4.

To make the pouches: Combine water and butter in a saucepan large enough to hold all the ingredients. Bring to the boil, stirring until the butter has melted. Remove from the heat, tip in all the flour and, using a wooden spoon, beat it well until the mixture comes cleanly away from the sides of the pan. Leave the mixture until it has cooled, then beat in the eggs. (You can use a food processor to beat in the eggs.)

Line a baking sheet with silicone paper. Either pipe or spoon the mixture into rounds about 2 cm (¾in) thick and 4 cm (1½in) in diameter. Bake for approximately 30 minutes. The pouches are ready when they are golden brown and the shell is firm and the inside hollow. Don't on any account open the oven door for the first 15 minutes. Slice the pouches in half immediately you take them from the oven.

While the pouches are baking make the filling as follows. Sauté the onion in the oil until it is soft but not coloured. Add the courgettes, aubergine, pepper, stir and cook with a lid on for two or three minutes. Then add the tomatoes, tomato purée and basil leaves. Season to taste with salt and pepper and simmer gently for 15 minutes.

Fill the pouches with the vegetable mixture and return to the oven for a few minutes to heat through before serving.

Potted Cheese

115g (4oz) mature cheddar, grated	250ml (½ pint) whipping cream
115g (4oz) Stilton cheese, grated	

Mix the cheeses with the cream, put in a china dish and microwave until the cheese has melted. Pour into individual ramekins and chill overnight.

Serve with Crusty Soda Bread and home-made pickle.

Crusty Soda Bread

675g (1½lb) wholemeal flour	225g (½lb) oatmeal
550g (1¼lb) plain flour	1 litre (1¾ pints) milk
20ml (4 teaspoons) cream of tartar	salt to taste
20ml (4 teaspoons) bicarbonate of soda	

Preheat oven: 180°C, 350°F; gas mark 4.

Sift the flours with the cream of tartar and bicarbonate of soda. Add the oatmeal and a pinch of salt. Make a well in the centre. Add the milk and mix to a dough. Knead well, then cut the dough into four. Mould each piece into a round and cut a deep cross in the top. Bake for approximately 35 minutes.

Summer Pudding

900g (2lb) mixed soft fruit, fresh or frozen. Blackcurrants are an essential, raspberries, strawberries, blueberries all taste good	225g (8oz) caster sugar
	½ a large thick sliced sandwich loaf, crusts removed

Bring fruit and sugar to the boil and simmer until the sugar is fully dissolved. Soak one side of each slice of bread in the juice and use it to line a 1·25 litre (2 pint) pudding basin, juice side out. Reserve 4 slices. Add half the fruit. Top it with a slice of bread, then put in the rest of the fruit. Place remaining bread on the top. Cover with a plate that fits and place a weight on the top. Chill in the fridge overnight.

To serve – unmould the pudding and decorate with some fresh raspberries or strawberries. Pouring cream, crème fraîche or yoghurt all complement summer pudding.

The National Trust Vegetarian Cooking Competition

In September 2001 The National Trust held its annual cooking competition. The theme for that year was Vegetarian Cooking, reflecting the growing demand from National Trust visitors for interesting vegetarian options on the Trust's restaurant and tea-shop menus.

The standard of the cooking was exceptional and the Trust's cooks held a vegetarian masterclass at Wimpole Hall, Cambridge-shire in the finals. As one of the judges, Orlando Murrin of the *BBC Good Food* magazine, commented, 'The standard of cookery is very, very high and the dishes are all colourful, imaginative and inspiring. None of them is old fashioned, in fact they are all state-of-the-art and dynamically modern.'

You may find the following three recipes to be a little more challenging than the other recipes in this book. However, take heart as all have been thoroughly tested before being published here. We recommend that you save these recipes for special occasions and allow yourself plenty of time for the preparation. None of the recipes is particularly difficult, but all of them have two or three different components that benefit from a little extra attention.

First Prize

Summer Vegetable and Goat's Cheese Parcels

Created by Sarah Bickford from Stourhead Landscape Garden

4–6 portions

Sarah made her own puff pastry for this delicious concoction and the recipe and method are given below, but if you are short of time the alternative is to use ready-made pastry.

Puff Pastry

450g (1lb) plain flour
450g (1lb) butter, cut into domino sized pieces
(300ml) 10 fl oz iced water
15ml lemon juice
pinch of salt

Alternatively use 680g (1·5lb) pack of ready-made puff pastry

Filling

225g (8oz) onion
225g (8oz) courgettes
100g (4oz) aubergines
½ a green pepper, de-seeded
½ a red pepper, de-seeded
½ a yellow pepper, de-seeded
3 plump cloves of garlic, finely chopped
15ml (1 tablespoon) vegetable oil
400g (14oz) tin chopped tomatoes
1 teaspoon caster sugar
1 teaspoon mixed dried herbs
100g (4oz) goat's cheese (Sarah used Wiltshire Rosary)
45ml (3 tablespoons) crème fraîche
salt and pepper to taste

To make the Pastry

Sift the flour and salt into a large mixing bowl. Add the butter and toss with the flour using a palette knife. Make a well in the centre and add the water and lemon juice. Mix gently with the palette knife to bring all ingredients together. Turn on to a floured board. Gently shape the mixture with your hands into a brick shape. Make three depressions widthways in the brick with a rolling pin. Roll the brick into an oblong approximately 33 cm (13 in) long and 20 cm (8 in) wide. Keep the board and rolling pin well floured while you are rolling and try to handle the pastry as little as possible. Fold one third over to the centre and the other third over the first two. Press the edges to trap the air in the block.

Rest the pastry for 5 minutes then give it one-quarter turn. Make the depressions as before, roll the block out again to the same size and fold again. Rest the pastry. Repeat this process a further four times. When finished, wrap and chill until required (preferably overnight). Bring to room temperature before the final rolling out.

To make the Filling

Finely chop all the vegetables. Heat the oil and garlic, sauté the onion for a minute or two to soften them, then add the rest of the vegetables, the tin of tomatoes, sugar and herbs and simmer for approximately half an hour. Crumble in the goat's cheese, add the crème fraîche, season and keep warm.

To Bake and Fill the Parcels

Preheat oven to 200°C, 400°F; gas mark 6.

Divide the pastry into four pieces. Roll out pieces to approximately 5 mm (¼ in) thick. You can leave the pieces as squares or cut out rounds of 15 cm (6 in). Decorate the shapes with any off-cuts; egg wash the parcel cases and place on baking paper on a baking sheet in a preheated oven. Bake for approximately 20 minutes until golden brown. If the bottoms are not crisping properly, turn the cases over for a few minutes until they do.

When they are cooked, cool until ready to handle, then split. If you find at this point that there is a little uncooked pastry inside the shell, scoop it out before filling with the warm cheese and vegetable mixture. Serve with an accompaniment of lightly dressed salad leaves.

Finn's Chilli Bean Bites with Champ and Spicy Pineapple Chutney

Created by Maire Murphy and Irene McAleese
from the Giant's Causeway

4 portions

I suggest preparing the Chilli Bean Bites and making the Pineapple Chutney ahead of time. This leaves plenty of time to fry the Bean Bites, make the Champ and dish up, just before eating.

For the Chilli Bean Bites

5ml olive oil
1 medium onion, peeled and finely chopped
2 garlic cloves, peeled and crushed
15ml (1 tablespoon), fresh mushrooms, chopped
15ml (1 tablespoon) gherkins, chopped

400g (14oz) can of red kidney beans, drained
1 level teaspoon chilli powder
50g (2oz) wholemeal breadcrumbs
1 egg
1 tablespoon fresh parsley chopped
1 tablespoon coriander chopped
salt and pepper to taste

For the Pineapple Chutney

225g (8oz) can of pineapple chunks in juice
15ml (1 tablespoon) sweet chilli sauce

15ml (1 tablespoon) balsamic vinegar
2 tablespoons caster sugar

For the Champ

2·7kg (6lbs) potatoes
1 bunch scallions (spring onions),
250ml (1 pint) milk

50g (2oz) butter
salt and pepper to taste

To prepare the Chilli Bean Bites

Heat the olive oil in a small pan and cook the onion, garlic and mushrooms until soft. Remove and transfer to the food processor. Add the gherkins, kidney beans, chilli powder, breadcrumbs, egg, parsley and coriander. Season to taste. Place in a food processor and pulse until combined keeping the mixture coarse. Shape the mixture into eight small cakes. Cover with cling film and chill until required.

To make the Pineapple Chutney

Dice the pineapple into small pieces and place in a small pan with the juice, chilli sauce, balsamic vinegar and the sugar. Bring to the boil and simmer until thick.

To make the Champ

Peel, chop and boil potatoes until soft. Drain. Heat the milk, butter and chopped scallions until boiling, simmer for 3 minutes and add to potatoes. Mix thoroughly and mash until smooth and fluffy. Keep warm until ready to serve.

Finally

Fry the Chilli Bean Bites in a little oil until brown and crisp. Allow two per person and serve with the warm Champ and the Pineapple Chutney as an accompaniment.

Third Prize

Spinach and Celeriac Bubble and Squeak with a Red Onion Marmalade finished with a Sweet Pepper Sauce and Carrot and Courgette Garnish

Created by Lee Underhill from Chartwell

4 portions

This recipe may appear dauntingly complicated but it is much easier than it seems as a lot of the preparation can be done ahead of time. I suggest preparing the Bubble and Squeak Cakes, the Red Onion Marmalade and the Sweet Pepper Sauce beforehand, leaving the final cooking of the cakes, roasting the accompanying vegetables and the assembly of the final dish to the last half hour or so before you want to serve it.

For the Bubble and Squeak
675g (1·5lbs) potatoes, peeled and diced
450g (1lb) celeriac peeled and diced
about 35g (1·5oz) butter, divided into three portions
45mls (3 tablespoons) milk
225g (8oz) fresh spinach, washed
salt, pepper and nutmeg to taste
15ml (1 tablespoon) olive oil

For the Red Onion Marmalade
275g (10oz) red onions, peeled and sliced
knob of butter
60mls (4 tablespoons) red wine vinegar
50g (2oz) dark brown sugar

For the Sweet Pepper Sauce
2 red peppers
15ml (1 tablespoon) chopped onion
15ml (1 tablespoon) olive oil
4-5 basil leaves
30mls (2 tablespoons) red wine vinegar
200mls (8 fl oz) vegetable stock

For the Garnish
250g (8oz) carrots, peeled and cut into batons
250g (8oz) courgettes, peeled and cut into batons
15ml (1 tablespoon) olive oil
small bunch of chives

Preheat oven 190°C, 375°F; gas mark 5.

To make the Bubble and Squeak
Place the diced potatoes and celeriac in a saucepan, cover with water, bring to the boil and simmer until soft, approximately 20-25 minutes. Drain and mash with one of the portions of butter and the milk. Place the spinach in a separate pan with the second portion of butter. Put a lid on the pan and allow the spinach to wilt. This will only take a minute or two. Drain the spinach and combine the two pans and season with salt, pepper and nutmeg to taste. Using a 10cm (4in) cutter, mould the mixture into cakes. Chill until required.

To make the Red Onion Marmalade
Sauté the onions gently in a knob of butter adding the red wine vinegar and the brown sugar. Simmer the mixture gently for approximately 25-30 minutes adding a little water if necessary until it reaches the consistency of a syrupy marmalade.

To make the Sweet Pepper Sauce

Slice and deseed peppers, lay on baking paper on a baking sheet and bake in oven until skin is blackened (approximately 20 minutes). Allow to cool until you can handle them, then peel and chop the peppers roughly and add to a small pan together with the onion and oil. Sauté gently for a couple of minutes, then add the basil leaves, the red wine vinegar and vegetable stock and simmer another 3–4 minutes. Remove from heat and liquidise.

To finish the Dish and make the Garnish

Bake the cakes in the oven as follows; place on baking paper on a baking tray and brush the cakes with a little oil. Alternatively, fry the cakes in 15ml (1 tablespoonful) of oil and the last portion of butter. In either case the cakes are ready when brown and crisp. Keep warm in the oven if necessary.

Par boil the carrots for 5 minutes, drain and place carrot and courgette batons on baking paper on a baking tray. Drizzle with olive oil and roast for 20 minutes in the oven.

To assemble the Dish

Reheat the Red Onion Marmalade and the Sweet Pepper Sauce. Place two Bubble and Squeak Cakes on each plate. Add a spoonful of marmalade on top of each cake. Divide the carrots and courgettes between the plates and drizzle over the Sweet Pepper Sauce. Garnish each plate with chopped chives, and serve immediately.

National Trust Restaurants and Tea-rooms

BERKSHIRE

Basildon Park
License applied for restaurant
Lower Basildon, Reading
RG8 9NR
Tel: (0118) 984 4080

Cliveden
Licensed restaurant
The Conservatory
Restaurant, Taplow,
Maidenhead SL6 0JA
Tel: (01628) 661406

BUCKINGHAMSHIRE

Hughenden Manor
Licensed restaurant
High Wycombe HP14 4LA
Tel: (01494) 755573

Stowe Gardens
Licensed tea-room
Buckingham MK18 5EH
Tel: (01280) 815819

Waddesdon Manor
Licensed restaurant
Waddesdon, near Aylesbury
HP18 0JH
Tel: (01296) 651211/282

CAMBRIDGESHIRE

Anglesey Abbey
Licensed restaurant
Lode, Cambridge
CB5 9EJ
Tel: (01223) 811175

Houghton Mill
Unlicensed restaurant
Houghton,
near Huntingdon
PE17 2AZ
Tel: (01480) 462413

Peckover House
Licensed tea-room
North Brink, Wisbech
PE13 1JR
Tel: (01945) 583463

Wicken Fen
Unlicensed kiosk
Lode Lane,
Wicken, Ely
CB7 5XP
Tel: (01353) 720274

Wimpole Hall
Licensed restaurant
The Old Rectory Restaurant,
Arrington,
near Royston
SG8 0BW
Tel: (01223) 208670

Wimpole Home Farm
Unlicensed café
Arrington,
near Royston
SG8 0BW
Tel: (01223) 208987

CHESHIRE

Dunham Massey
Licensed restaurant
The Stables Restaurant,
near Altrincham
WA14 4SJ
Tel: (0161) 941 2815

Little Moreton Hall
Licensed restaurant
near Congleton
CW12 4SD
Tel: (01260) 272018

Lyme Park
Licensed tea-room
Disley, Stockport
SK12 2NX
Tel: (01663) 762023

CORNWALL

Carnewas
near Bedruthan Steps
Unlicensed tea-room
Carnewas Tea-room,
St Eval, Wadebridge
PL27 7UW
Tel: (01637) 860701

Cotehele
Licensed restaurant
St Dominick, Saltash
PL12 6TA
Tel: (01579) 352711

Public House
The Edgcumbe Arms,
The Quay, Cotehele,
St Dominick, Saltash
PL12 6TA
Tel: (01579) 350024

Lanhydrock
Licensed restaurant
Bodmin PL30 5AD
Tel: (01208) 74331

St Michael's Mount
Licensed restaurant
The Sail Loft Restaurant,
Marazion TR17 0HT
Tel: (01736) 710748

Trelissick Garden
Licensed restaurant
Feock, Truro TR3 6QL
Tel: (01872) 863486

Trerice
Licensed tea-room
Kestle Mill, Newquay
TR8 4PG
Tel: (01673) 875404

CUMBRIA

Acorn Bank
Licensed tea-room
Temple Sowerby,
near Penrith
CA10 1SP
Tel: (017683) 61893

Fell Foot Park
Licensed tea-room
Newby Bridge, Ulverston
LA12 8NN
Tel: (015395) 31273

Sizergh Castle
Licensed tea-room
near Kendal LA8 8AE
Tel: (015395) 60070

Wordsworth House
Licensed tea-room
Main Street, Cockermouth
CA13 9RX
Tel: (01900) 824820

DERBYSHIRE

Calke Abbey
Licensed restaurant
The Threshing Barn
Restaurant, Ticknall
DE73 1LE
Tel: (01332) 864803

Hardwick Hall
Licensed restaurant
The Great Kitchen
Restaurant, Doe Lea,
Chesterfield S44 5QJ
Tel: (01246) 854088

Ilam Hall
Unlicensed tea-room
The Manifold Tea-room,
Ilam, Ashbourne
DE6 2AZ
Tel: (01335) 350245

Kedleston Hall
Licensed restaurant
Derby DE22 5JH
Tel: (01332) 842191

Longshaw
Unlicensed tea-room
Longshaw Information
Centre, Sheffield
S11 7TZ
Tel: (01433) 631708

Sudbury Hall
Licensed tea-room
The Coach House Tea-room,
Sudbury DE6 5HT
Tel: (01283) 585337

DEVON

Arlington Court
Licensed restaurant
near Barnstaple EX31 4LP
Tel: (01271) 850629

Buckland Abbey
Licensed restaurant
Yelverton, Plymouth
PL20 6EY
Tel: (01822) 855024

Castle Drogo
Licensed restaurant
Drewsteignton EX6 6PB
Tel: (01647) 432629

Finch Foundry
Unlicensed tea-room
Sticklepath, Okehampton
EX20 2NW
Tel: (01837) 840046

Killerton
*Licensed self-service
restaurant*
Broadclyst EX5 3LE
Tel: (01392) 882081

Knightshayes Court
*Licensed self-service
restaurant*
Bolham, Tiverton EX16 7RQ
Tel: (01884) 259416

Lydford Gorge
Unlicensed tea-room
The Stables, Lydford,
Okehampton EX20 4BH
Tel: (01822) 820441

Overbecks
Unlicensed tea-room
Sharpitor, Salcombe
TQ8 8LW
Tel: (01548) 842893

Saltram House
Licensed restaurant
Plympton, Plymouth
PL7 1UH
Tel: (01752) 340635

Watersmeet House
Unlicensed tea-room
Watersmeet Rd, Lynmouth
EX35 6NT
Tel: (01598) 753348

DORSET

Brownsea Island
Unlicensed tea-room
Café Villano, Poole Harbour
BH15 7EE
Tel: (01202) 700244

Corfe Castle
Licensed tea-room
The Castle Tea-room,
The Square, near Wareham
BH20 5EZ
Tel: (01929) 481332

Kingston Lacy
Licensed restaurant
Wimborne Minster
BH21 4EA
Tel: (01202) 889242

Studland
Unlicensed tea-room
Knoll Beach Café,
Knoll Beach BH19 3AX
Tel: (01929) 450305

EAST SUSSEX

Bateman's
Licensed tea-room
Burwash, Etchingham
TN19 7DS
Tel: (01435) 882302

Bodiam Castle
Unlicensed tea-room
Wharfside Tea-room,
near Robertsbridge
TN32 5VA
Tel: (01580) 830074

ESSEX

Flatford: Bridge Cottage
Licensed tea-room
Flatford, East Bergholt,
Colchester CO7 6OL
Tel: (01206) 298260

Hatfield Forest
Unlicensed tea-room
Lakeside Café, Takeley,
Bishop's Stortford
CM22 6NE
Tel: (01279) 870579

GATESHEAD

Gibside
Unlicensed tea-room
near Rowlands Gill,
Burnopfield,
Newcastle upon Tyne
NE16 6BG
Tel: (01207) 545801

GLOUCESTERSHIRE

Dyrham Park
Licensed restaurant
Chippenham
SN14 8ER
Tel: (0117) 9374293

Hidcote Manor Garden
*Licensed restaurant and
unlicensed tea-room*
The Garden Restaurant,
Hidcote Bartrim,
near Chipping Campden
GL55 6LR
Tel: (01386) 438703

HAMPSHIRE

Mottisfont Abbey
Licensed restaurant
Mottisfont, near Romsey
SO51 0LP
Tel: (01794) 340757

The Vyne
Licensed restaurant
The Old Brewhouse
Restaurant,
Sherborne St John,
Basingstoke RG24 9HL
Tel: (01256) 880039

HERTFORDSHIRE

Ashridge Estate
Unlicensed kiosk
The National Trust Visitor
Centre, Ringshall,
Berkhamsted
HP4 1LT
Tel: (01442) 851227

ISLE OF WIGHT

The Needles Old Battery
Unlicensed tea-room
West Highdown,
Totland PO39 0JH
Tel: (01983) 754772

KENT

Chartwell
Licensed restaurant
Westerham TN16 1PS
Tel: (01732) 863087

Emmetts Garden
Licensed restaurant
Ide Hill, Sevenoaks
TN14 6AY
Tel: (01732) 863087

Ightham Mote
Unlicensed tea-room
Ivy Hatch, Sevenoaks
TN15 0NT
Tel: (01732) 811314

Knole
Unlicensed tea-room
Brewhouse Tea-room,
Sevenoaks
TN15 0RP
Tel: (01732) 741762

**The White Cliffs
of Dover**
Unlicensed tea-room
Langdon Cliffs, near Dover
CT16 1HJ
Tel: (01304) 202756

**Sissinghurst Castle
Garden**
Licensed restaurant
The Granary Restaurant,
Sissinghurst,
near Cranbrook TN17 2AB
Tel: (01580) 710704

LANCASHIRE

Rufford Old Hall
Licensed restaurant
Rufford, near Ormskirk
L40 1SG
Tel: (01704) 821254

LINCOLNSHIRE

Belton House
Licensed restaurant
The Stables Restaurant
Belton, Grantham
NG32 2LS
Tel: (01476) 573086

LIVERPOOL

Speke Hall
*Licensed (wine only)
tea-room*
The Walk L24 1XD
Tel: (0151) 427 7231

LONDON

Osterley Park
Licensed restaurant
Isleworth TW7 4RB
Tel: (020) 8569 7624

Sutton House
Licensed café/bar
2 & 4 Homerton High Street,
Hackney E9 6JQ
Tel: (020) 8525 9052

MIDDLESBROUGH

Ormesby Hall
Unlicensed tea-room
Middlesbrough
TS7 9AS
Tel: (01642) 324188

NORFOLK

Blickling Hall
Licensed restaurant
Blickling, Norwich
NR11 6NF
Tel: (01263) 738046

Felbrigg Hall
Licensed restaurant
The Park Restaurant,
Felbrigg NR11 8PR
Tel: (01263) 838237

Oxburgh Hall
Licensed restaurant
Oxborough, King's Lynn
PE33 9PS
Tel: (01366) 328258

NORTHAMPTONSHIRE

Canons Ashby House
Unlicensed tea-room
The Brewhouse Tea-room,
Canons Ashby, Daventry
NN11 3SD
Tel: (01327) 860044

NORTHERN IRELAND

The Argory
Unlicensed tea-room
Moy, Dungannon,
Co. Tyrone BT71 6NA
Tel: (028) 8778 4753

Crom Estate
Unlicensed tea-room
Newtownbutler,
Co. Fermanagh
BT92 8AP
Tel: (028) 6773 8118

Castle Ward
Unlicensed restaurant
Strangford, Downpatrick,
Co. Down
BT30 7LS
Tel: (028) 4488 1204

Giant's Causeway
Unlicensed restaurant
The Giant's Pantry
44a Causeway Road,
Bushmills,
Co. Antrim
BT57 8SU
Tel: (028) 2073 2972

Mount Stewart
Unlicensed tea-room
The Ark Club Tea Room,
Portaferry Road,
Newtownards,
Co. Down
BT22 2AD
Tel: (028) 4278 8801

Springhill
Unlicensed tea-room
20 Springhill Rd,
Moneymore,
Magherafelt,
Co. Londonderry
BT45 7NQ
Tel: (028) 8674 8210

NORTHUMBERLAND

Cragside
Licensed restaurant
The Vickers Rooms
Restaurant, Rothbury,
Morpeth
NE65 7PX
Tel: (01669) 620134

**Hadrian's Wall
& Housesteads Fort**
*Unlicensed refreshments
kiosk*
Bardon Mill, Hexham
NE47 6NN
Tel: (01434) 344525

Wallington
*Unlicensed self-service
restaurant*
Pipers Room,
Cambo, Morpeth
NE61 4AR
Tel: (01670) 774274

NOTTINGHAMSHIRE

Clumber Park
*Licensed restaurant and
tea-room*
Worksop S80 3AZ
Tel: (01909) 484122

OXFORDSHIRE

Greys Court
Unlicensed tea-room
Rotherfield Greys,
Henley-on-Thames
RG9 4PG
Tel: (01491) 628529

Upton House
Unlicensed tea-room
Banbury OX15 6HT
Tel: (01295) 670266

SHROPSHIRE

Attingham Park
Licensed tea-room
Shrewsbury SY4 4TP
Tel: (01743) 709203

Carding Mill Valley
Unlicensed café
Chalet Pavilion,
Church Stretton
SY6 6JG
Tel: (01694) 722631

Dudmaston
Unlicensed tea-room
Quatt, Bridgnorth
WV15 6QN
Tel: (01746) 780866

SOMERSET

Barrington Court
Licensed restaurant
near Ilminster
TA19 0NQ
Tel: (01460) 241244

Montacute House
Licensed restaurant
Montacute
TA15 6XP
Tel: (01935) 826294

Tintinhull
Unlicensed tea-room
Stable Tea-Rooms,
Farm Street, Yeovil
BA22 9PZ
Tel: (01935) 826294

SUFFOLK

Dunwich Heath
Licensed tea-room
Coastguard Cottages,
Dunwich,
Saxmundham
IP17 3DJ
Tel: (01728) 648505

Ickworth
Licensed restaurant
Horringer,
Bury St Edmunds
IP29 5QE
Tel: (01284) 735086

Lavenham Guildhall
Unlicensed tea-room
Market Place,
Lavenham, Sudbury
CO10 9QZ
Tel: (01787) 247646

STAFFORDSHIRE

Biddulph Grange Garden
Unlicensed tea-room
Stoke on Trent
ST8 7SD
Tel: (01782) 517999

Moseley Old Hall
Licensed tea-room
Fordhouses,
Wolverhampton
WV10 7HY
Tel: (01902) 782808

Wightwick Manor
Unlicensed tea-room
Wightwick Bank,
Wolverhampton
WV6 8EE
Tel: (01902) 761108

SUNDERLAND

Souter Lighthouse
Unlicensed tea-room
Coast Road, Whitburn
SR6 7NH
Tel: (0191) 5293161

SURREY

Box Hill
Unlicensed open-air café
The Old Fort,
Tadworth, near Dorking
KT20 7LB
Tel: (01306) 888793

**Claremont Landscape
Garden**
Unlicensed tea-room
Portsmouth Road,
Esher KT10 9JG
Tel: (01372) 469421

Ham House
Licensed tea-room
The Orangery Tea-Room,
Ham, Richmond
TW10 7RS
Tel: (020) 8940 0735

Morden Hall Park
Licensed café
The Riverside Café,
Morden Hall Road,
Morden SM4 5JD
Tel: (020) 8687 0881

Polesden Lacey
Licensed tea-room
Great Bookham,
near Dorking
RH5 6BD
Tel: (01372) 456190

Winkworth Arboretum
Unlicensed tea-room
Hascombe Road,
Godalming GU8 4AD
Tel: (01483) 208265

WALES

Chirk Castle
Licensed tea-room
Chirk
LL14 5AF
Tel: (01691) 773279

Erddig
Licensed restaurant
Wrexham
LL13 0YT
Tel: (01978) 315184

Penrhyn Castle
Licensed tea-room
Bangor,
Gwynedd
LL57 4HN
Tel: (01248) 371381

Plas Newydd
Licensed restaurant
Llanfairpwll,
Anglesey
LL61 6DQ
Tel: (01248) 716848

Powis Castle
Licensed tea-room
Welshpool,
Powys
SY21 8RF
Tel: (01938) 555499

WARWICKSHIRE

Baddesley Clinton
Licensed restaurant
The Barn Restaurant,
Rising Lane,
Knowle, Solihull
B93 0DQ
Tel: (01564) 785569

Charlecote Park
Unlicensed restaurant
The Orangery Restaurant,
Warwick CV35 9ER
Tel: (01789) 470448

WEST SUSSEX

Nymans Gardens
Licensed tea-room
The Pavilion Restaurant,
Handcross,
near Haywards Heath
RH17 6EB
Tel: (01444) 400161

Petworth House
Licensed restaurant
Petworth GU28 0AE
Tel: (01798) 344975

Standen
Licensed restaurant
The Barn Restaurant,
East Grinstead RH19 4NE
Tel: (01342) 323029

Uppark
Licensed restaurant
South Harting, Petersfield
GU31 5QR
Tel: (01730) 825256

WILTSHIRE

Stourhead
Unlicensed tea-room
Village Hall Tea Rooms,
Stourton, Warminster
BA12 6QD
Tel: (01747) 840161

WORCESTERSHIRE

Hanbury Hall
Unlicensed tea-room
Droitwich WR9 7EA
Tel: (01527) 821214

Snowshill Manor
*Restaurant (Applying
for license)*
Piper's Grove Restaurant,
Broadway WR12 7JU
Tel: (01386) 858685

YORKSHIRE

Beningbrough Hall
Licensed restaurant
Shipton,
Beningbrough
YO30 1DD
Tel: (01904) 470513

East Riddlesden Hall
Unlicensed tea-room
The National Trust
Tea Room,
Bradford Road,
Keighley
BD20 5EL
Tel: (01535) 607075

**Fountains Abbey and
Studley Royal**
*Licensed restaurant and
tea-room*
Ripon HG4 3DY
Tel: (01765) 601003

Nostell Priory
Licensed tea-room
Doncaster Road,
Nostell,
near Wakefield
WF4 1QE
Tel: (01924) 863892

Nunnington Hall
Unlicensed tea-room
Nunnington
YO62 5UY
Tel: (01439) 748283

Treasurer's House
Licensed tea-room
Minster Yard,
York YO1 7JL
Tel: (01904) 646757

York Tea-Room
Licensed tea-room
30 Goodramgate,
York YO1 7LG
Tel: (01904) 659282

Index